100 THINGS TO DO IN SARASOTA BEFORE YOU DIE

100 THINGS TO DO IN SARASOTA BEFORE YOU DIE

KELLY STILWELL

Fish sandwich from Shore

100 THINGS TO DO IN SARASOTA BEFORE YOU DIE

KELLY STILWELL

Reedy Press
PO Box 5131
St. Louis, MO 63139, USA
reedypress.com

Library of Congress Control Number: 2024939004

ISBN: 9781681065427

Design by Jill Halpin

All photos are courtesy of the author unless otherwise noted.

Printed in the United States of America
25 26 27 28   5 4 3

DEDICATION

To my husband, Tim, who understands my love for travel and writing and always supports me in both.

To my daughters, Taylor and Jessie, who are always ready to go exploring with me.

Fish sandwich from Shore

CONTENTS

Music and Entertainment

Sports and Recreation

Culture and History

Shopping and Fashion

ACKNOWLEDGMENTS

Thank you to those who shared their love of the Sarasota-Bradenton area with me as I was writing this book.

To Visit Sarasota, specifically to Olivia Turpening, I so appreciate all your suggestions and introductions.

To Paula Wright, owner and editor of *Bradenton Magazine*, your love for our area inspires me, and I treasure your friendship.

To Reedy Press, thank you for choosing me to write this book about my home!

To the Reedy Press authors group, I'm grateful for your willingness to share your ideas.

PREFACE

What a blessing to live in this part of the world. As a travel writer who has visited 40 countries, I always feel so good when returning to the Sarasota-Bradenton area. After visiting family in Siesta Key for years when our girls were little, we finally bit the bullet and moved to Bradenton in 2009. We have never looked back and absolutely love our life here.

I started my website, Food, Fun & Faraway Places, not long after moving to Bradenton. I've always had a love for writing, so to be able to write about food and travel was a dream come true. I'm now a contributor to *USA Today* 10Best, MSN, and *Bradenton Magazine*, as well as a guest travel pro on *Suncoast View*, the local morning show. I share my adventures with over 350,000 followers between Instagram (@kastilwell), Pinterest (kastilwell), and Facebook (KellyAStilwell).

Sarasota was ranked the #1 place to live in Florida in 2023 by *U.S. News & World Report*, and the #5 place to live in the US, so if you live here, you've chosen well. When I started exploring our little part of the world, little did I know how much there was to see and do right here at home. With an average of 255 days of sunshine per year, there's plenty of time to get outside and play!

We, like many of you, were drawn to this area because of the beach. Whether you visit the laid-back beaches of Anna Maria Island, the secluded beaches of Longboat Key, or the expansive and busier beaches of Siesta Key—they each have their charm.

People flock to the Sarasota-Bradenton region for the glorious weather, and we have a lot of activities to keep you busy. Start your day by kayaking the mangroves, paddleboarding on the Sarasota Bay, taking a beach yoga class, or relaxing on one of our beaches with calm, clear waters. Prefer a hike? Check out Celery Fields at sunrise.

After you've worked up an appetite, enjoy lunch at one of our fabulous restaurants, including many with a view of the Gulf of Mexico.

Afternoons are made for exploring, and where else can you see an entire circus in miniature, a world-class art gallery, and the home that John Ringling built for his wife Mable, all within a few hours?

When I moved here, I had no idea what an incredible arts scene we had here on the Gulf Coast. From an award-winning symphony to spectacular hit musicals, as well as the largest professional theater in the Southeastern United States, we really do have it all.

This time, like all times, is a very good one, if we but know what to do with it.—Ralph Waldo Emerson

I hope this book of *100 Things to Do in Sarasota Before You Die* helps you discover more things to do with your time, and that your time here is a very good one.

Tide Tables

FOOD AND DRINK

1

CHOOSE YOUR OWN CHARCUTERIE BOARD

AT CHÂTEAU 13

Charcuterie has been überpopular for the last few years, and at Château 13 you can build your own from the list of meats, cheeses, and condiments. Owner Wim Lippens came to Bradenton as an exchange student from Belgium when he was in high school in the early '90s. From that time, he knew he wanted to move to Manatee County. Lucky for us, the Lippens family moved here and started a B and B in Palmetto, which led to them opening Château 13. Why should you visit? The food is exceptional, from the cheese and charcuterie offerings, which change daily, to the Chef's Prix Fixe (signature menu) to the outstanding burgers and hand-cut fries. You can't go wrong with anything on the menu. Whether you want to dress up for date night, sit at the bar and have appetizers and wine, or come as you are for The Louis XIII Burger, you're sure to fall in love with Château 13.

535 13th St. W, Bradenton, 941-226-0110
chateau-13.com

TIP

Why not order ahead? Pick up a charcuterie meal and take it to the Riverwalk or beach for sunset.

EAT WITH THE SEASONS
AT INDIGENOUS

This upscale restaurant in Sarasota is known for seasonal produce and sustainable seafood, working with local fishermen and farmers as much as possible. In fact, most days the chefs are on farms picking vegetables for the dishes they will be serving that day. Dining at Indigenous is not just eating out, it's an experience. Chef Steve Phelps was a semifinalist for the James Beard Foundation Best Chef: South award, and it's easy to see why. He changes the menu regularly, showcasing ingredients at their peak. The wild mushroom bisque with truffle oil and rye croutons is one of the most popular appetizers. The seafood is always outstanding. Try the scallops or one of the fish dishes. For those who aren't seafood fans, I hope My Uncles Burger with bacon jam and those duck fat roasted potatoes is on the menu. Make sure to save room for dessert. You're welcome.

239 S Links Ave., 941-706-4740
indigenoussarasota.com

3

GRAB A BURGER ON THE BEACH

AT SKINNY'S PLACE

What could be better than a burger on the beach? A burger with an ice-cold beer or soda on the beach! Carl "Skinny" Freeman and his wife, Janice, bought this little piece of land in 1952 and built the Mid-Island Drive In, knowing Anna Maria Island would one day be a popular tourist destination. Pretty smart move. This wonderful little spot was renamed Skinny's Place in Grandpa Skinny's honor. Order a burger—they're all quarter-pounders and come with fixings and pickles on the side. Other sandwiches and fried chicken are also on the menu. There's even a veggie option. We always go for the burger, believing it's what Grandpa Skinny would have wanted. We order it with extra tomato, onion rings, and a bottle of Coca-Cola, just like Grandma Skinny. Toes in sand, burger in hand—that's the way we roll.

3901 Gulf Dr., Holmes Beach, 941-778-7769
skinnysplace.com

OTHER PLACES FOR A GREAT BURGER

3 Keys Brewing & Gastrobrew
2505 Manatee Ave. E, Bradenton, 941-218-0396
3keysbrewing.com

Central Cafe
906 Manatee Ave. E, Bradenton, 941-757-0050
centralcafe941.com

Duffy's Tavern
5808 Marina Dr., Holmes Beach, 941-778-2501
duffystavernami.com

Michael John's
1040 Carlton Arms Blvd., Bradenton, 941-747-8032
michaeljohnsrestaurant.com

New Pass Grill & Bait Shop
1505 Ken Thompson Pkwy., 941-388-3050
newpassgrill.com

Patricks 1481
1481 Main St., 941-955-1481
patricks1481.com

Shake Pit
3801 Manatee Ave. W, Bradenton, 941-748-4016

State Street Eating House
1533 State St., 941-951-1533
statestreetsrq.com

4

TASTE THE FLAVORS OF PERU
AT SELVA

If you'd like to taste the flavors of Peru without making the 2,500-mile trip, it doesn't get much more authentic than the Latin fusion at Selva Grill. Peruvian food is unique with its spices of huacatay, aji amarillo, and chinco, though it's not necessarily a spicy cuisine. We'd suggest you begin with the pisco sour, a classic Peruvian cocktail. For an appetizer, you've got to try the macadamia-pesto-encrusted sea scallops, any of their ceviches, or one of the varieties of empanadas. We usually share two to three appetizers in lieu of an entrée, but the mirin-roasted sea bass is hard to resist. And don't forget dessert as Selva Grill shines here, too. You really can't go wrong with anything on the menu, and every dish is Instagram-worthy. For those who have been to Peru, you won't find guinea pig on this menu, and we're not mad about it!

1345 Main St., 941-362-4427
67 N Cattlemen Rd., 941-358-6272
selvagrill.com

Each year in June during Savor Sarasota, dozens of restaurants offer a prix-fixe menu that will save you a bundle. This is a great time to check out restaurants like Selva, which you might otherwise reserve for a really special occasion.

visitsarasota.com/savor-sarasota

5

EAT THE FRESHEST SEAFOOD RIGHT OFF THE BOAT

AT STAR FISH COMPANY

At Star Fish Company, you'll be eating the freshest seafood, almost all harvested by Florida's commercial fishermen. Started in the 1920s as a wholesale fishing business, it changed hands in the '50s and again in 1996. That year the owner started offering cooked food, and the restaurant was born. The menu has a lot of choices, including appetizers, soups, salads, and plenty of entrées. Grab a picnic table and enjoy your basket of grouper tacos or Gulf shrimp served with hush puppies and a side. Take in the view of the mangrove islands and Bradenton Beach. This is Florida at its best. You might just see the biggest catch of the day come in. See something you like? Head to the market after your meal and pick up something to take home. Their "chalkboard" is updated as soon as something comes in, so you can easily see what's available. Whether you're dining in or taking it away, bring cash as Star Fish doesn't accept credit cards.

12306 46th Ave. W, Cortez, 941-794-1243
starfishcompany.com

6

DINE IN ELEGANCE WITH YOUR TOES IN THE SAND

AT BEACH BISTRO

Beach Bistro is a special-occasion restaurant for most. The Bistro Experience menu is pricey but worth it. Dining here truly is an experience—from the Little Cocktail as part of the First Taste to the Key lime pie, an option in Course Four, you won't be disappointed. In between, choose from a plethora of dishes like grouper Floribbean, Maple Leaf Farms duckling breast, or American Ranchlands domestic lamb. There's also an optional upgrade to Food Heaven, a replica of the menu served by Beach Bistro at the James Beard House in 2005, with another option of a wine pairing. By the way, pace yourself. It's a lot of food and you may want to box some of it up to take home. Whether you choose the inside dining room or a table outside in the sand, the waitstaff is always exceptional, making you feel as if you're the only one there. Reservations are required.

6600 Gulf Dr., Holmes Beach, 941-778-6444
beachbistro.com

TIP

Sign up for the Beach Bistro mailing list and you'll receive a glass of bubbly with your meal on your birthday or anniversary.

7

DROP IN FOR A BITE
AT NEW PASS GRILL & BAIT SHOP

If you're looking for Old Florida vibes, head to the New Pass Grill & Bait Shop. Located right on Sarasota Bay, this is a one-stop shop for anything you need for a day on the water, from bait and fishing charters to award-winning burgers. The Grill serves breakfast, lunch, and dinner, and has beer and wine as well. We recommend the New Pass Famous Angus Burger and a side of onion rings, but they have plenty of other offerings. The blackened grouper sandwich is pretty amazing, too. When you arrive, just mosey on up to the window and place your order. Find a picnic table and wait until they call your name. It's worth the wait. My daughter volunteered at Mote Marine Aquarium (just around the corner), and my husband always offered to take her to her shift so he could stop at New Pass Grill for their famous breakfast sandwich.

1505 Ken Thompson Pkwy., 941-388-3050
newpassgrill.com

8

WATCH THE SUNSET FROM YOUR TABLE IN THE SAND

AT SANDBAR

Sandbar Seafood & Spirits has been a favorite of my family since before we moved to the Sunshine State. Situated right on the beach on the Gulf of Mexico, the location couldn't be more perfect. Over the years there were different owners, but in 1979 Ed Chiles bought Sandbar with plans to serve great food with an amazing view. We've been visiting Sandbar for over 20 years and can testify that Chiles has done exactly what he said he would do. With dishes like coconut shrimp, fish tacos, and epic burgers, you really can't go wrong with anything on the menu. There is plenty of outside seating, but even more inside tables for those days when it's just too hot to sit outside. Oftentimes when a restaurant has a location like this, the food doesn't have to be great to keep them busy. Sandbar has both the view and the food.

100 Spring Ave., Anna Maria, 941-778-0444
sandbardining.com

9

GRAB A SEAT AT THE BAR

AT SPEAKS CLAM BAR

Having appetizers at the bar is one of our favorite ways to spend date night, and the bartenders at Speaks Clam Bar always make us feel at home. The menu is full of amazing seafood dishes, as you'd expect from a place called Clam Bar, but the kitchen makes fresh pasta and the Italian dishes are always delicious with large portions. We're not usually creatures of habit, unless we're at Speaks. We start with the smoked fish dip followed by crispy eggplant Napoleon, both so good we've ordered them again back-to-back and couldn't eat another thing! Usually, our willpower is strong enough that we're able to order our other favorites, the steamed PEI mussels for my husband and the shrimp and clam bowl for me. Order a drink, settle in, and take your time deciding what to order. The menu is long, and you just might have to come back if you can't fit it all in the first time.

29 N Blvd. of the Presidents, 941-232-7633
8764 E SR 70, Lakewood Ranch, 941-232-7646
speaksclambar.com

10

DINE ON FRESH SEAFOOD
AT LUCKY PELICAN BISTRO

Lucky Pelican is another hidden gem, but once you find it, you'll be a regular. You won't find a nice view here, but the food makes up for it. The cuisine has a New England coastal flair, with a focus on seafood. Start with something from the raw bar, or try the mussels Rockefeller or peel-and-eat shrimp. Though we have tried just about everything on the menu, fish is where Lucky Pelican really excels. From the starter of fish dip to the beer-battered fish-and chips, Lucky Pelican does fish so well. My favorites are either the sake-glazed sea bass or the roasted cod. Both come with the most delightful veggie pancakes and tempura veggies. You probably won't be able to finish it, so ask for a box. I ate it cold the next day and it was still so delicious. Ask about the day's specials.

6239 Lake Osprey Dr., 941-907-0589
luckypelicanbistro.com

11

PRACTICE YOUR CHOPSTICKS SKILLS

AT MATAKA JAPANESE RAMEN HOUSE

Authentic Japanese ramen in Bradenton? See for yourself at Mataka. This small ramen house is tucked away in the Northwest Promenade strip center in west Bradenton. We were skeptical, too, but this has become one of our favorite spots, especially after a beach day. If you haven't been to a ramen house before, the servers can help you decide on the type of broth. Once you make that decision, choose from the ramen dishes with that broth. Noodles are straight, wavy, or udon style, which is a thicker noodle. If ramen isn't your thing, not to worry! You'll find several rice bowls like curry chicken rice. Check out the variety of steam buns. The fried chicken steam bun is a favorite! Start with an appetizer like Pork Gyoza (pan-fried dumplings) or steam buns to share while you decide. Mataka serves a variety of beers, sakes, and soft drinks. Kids will love the Ramune Japanese sodas.

6749 Manatee Ave., Bradenton, 941-896-3552
mitakaramen.com

12

CELEBRATE OLD FLORIDA CHARM
AT THE COTTAGE

Located in the heart of Siesta Key Village, The Cottage serves up some of the best food in the area in a charming atmosphere. Request a table in the back garden for an island vibe. There are two outdoor patios, or you can dine inside at a table or the bar. Though the atmosphere is fun and relaxing, the food is going to blow you away. Our favorites are from the tapas menu, like the short rib bites served in a crispy onion crust or wonton tuna tacos served in a wonton shell. The Cottage crab cakes are amazing, as well. Moving on to the entrées, your choices are dishes like lobster maki sushi, which is surf and turf with a twist; seafood scampi; or a perfectly cooked filet mignon. Rather have a burger or a chicken sandwich? You can get that, too. Start with the Cottage Cocktail or a glass of wine from their list. And don't forget dessert!

153 Avineda Messina, 941-312-9300
cottagesiestakey.com

13

ENJOY COFFEE, BREAKFAST, AND DESSERT
AT OF KORS BAKERY

Owners Alex and Marie Korsykov came to the US from Ukraine in 2013. The couple says their mission is to create delicious memories. I think anyone who walks into Of Kors Bakery would say they are doing just that. This bright and charming bakery located in downtown Sarasota offers up a variety of teas and caffeine in many forms, but the stars of the show are the baked goods and desserts. They begin the baking each day at 4 a.m., using mostly organic ingredients. They work with local farmers to source locally. You can watch (and smell!) the baking through the open kitchen. When you're ready to order, choose from cinnamon rolls, muffins, choux, meringue tarts, pavlova, éclairs, and yes, even more. Try the Slavic crepes, a savory stuffed bagel sandwich, or a chicken salad crepe with spinach and mozzarella. Fresh-squeezed orange juice is also available.

1359 Main St., 941-330-2220
ofkorsbakery.com

OTHER GREAT BREAKFAST SPOTS

Atria Cafe
4120 Lakewood Ranch Blvd., Lakewood Ranch, 941-751-1016
atria.cafe

Blue Dolphin Cafe
470 John Ringling Blvd., 941-388-3566
5370 Gulf of Mexico Dr., Ste. 101, Longboat Key, 941-383-3787
bluedolphincafe.com

Ginny & Jane E's Cafe and Coastal Store
9807 Gulf Dr., Anna Maria, 941-778-3170
ginnysandjanees.com

Harry's Continental Kitchens
5600 Gulf of Mexico Dr., Longboat Key, 941-383-0777
harryskitchen.com

Sage Biscuit Café
1401 Manatee Ave. W, Bradenton, 941-405-4744
6656 Cortez Rd. W, Bradenton, 941-792-3970
sagebiscuitbradenton.com

The Breakfast House
1817 Fruitville Rd., 941-366-6860
sarasotabreakfasthouse.com

Station 400
400 N Lemon Ave., 941-906-1400
8215 Lakewood Main St., Ste. P103, Lakewood Ranch, 941-907-0648
station400.com

The Granary
2547 Lakewood Ranch Blvd., Lakewood Ranch, 941-746-2000
thegranarylwr.com

14

EAT LIKE A SOUTHERNER
AT OWEN'S FISH CAMP

Owen's Fish Camp brings in local fish from the bay every single day, so if you want some of the freshest fish around, this is your spot. A Southern-inspired "seafood joint," Owen's has a laid-back, fun atmosphere. Start with their deviled eggs with "Redneck Caviar," hot crab dip, or a bowl of mussels with melted leek broth. The salads are large and creative and pair well with their Wicked Good New England Clam Chowda or spicy gumbo. Love your seafood fried? Choose from one of the baskets. Two can share the Low Country Boil with snow crab legs, shrimp, clams, mussels, and andouille sausage. Sandwiches are typical Southern menu choices, served with Old Bay fries or slaw. For an entrée, we go with the shrimp and grits with spicy smoked sausage or the spicy jambalaya with shrimp, chicken, and andouille sausage, crawfish, and dirty rice. That's good eatin' right there.

516 Burns Ct., 941-951-6936
6516 University Pkwy., Lakewood Ranch, 941-951-5052
owensfishcamp.com

TIP

Owen's does not accept reservations. Especially during high season, arrive early or your wait could be long.

15

RESERVE A TABLE IN THE WINE CAVE
AT CAFÉ GABBIANO

Café Gabbiano had me at wine cave. There's also a wine room, which is equally lovely. Either way, you are surrounded by wine selected by Marc Grimaud, one of the owners, who just happens to be a sommelier as well. Simply ask, and Marc will pair a wine with your meal. Head chef Paolo Di Costanzo hails from a small island off the coast of Naples, Italy. He's creative and uses only the best ingredients. Try one of the dishes made with their handmade pasta, like the truffle Sacchettini or the lobster ravioli. Prefer gnocchi? It's hand rolled, and the chef prepares the special gnocchi dish daily. We started with the chef's choice formaggi and salumi plate, which held a selection of cheeses, prosciutto, and speck, paired with warm olives and bruschetta with tomatoes, served with bread and truffle honey. It was heavenly. With 10 sweet endings on the dessert menu, you really should order at least one to share.

5104 Ocean Blvd., 941-349-1423
cafegabbiano.com

16

FEAST ON TRADITIONAL INDIAN FOOD

AT TANDOOR SARASOTA

We discovered Tandoor shortly after moving to the area. This popular family-owned restaurant has been serving authentic Indian food since 2001, which explains all the people patiently waiting outside for their turn to taste it. Start with the Tandoor Sampler so you can taste the samosas, pakoras, chicken tikka, and seekh kabab. For entrées, the curry is exceptional, a treasured family recipe using garlic, ginger, onions, tomatoes, and fresh-ground spices. You choose the heat, from mild to hot. The butter chicken is a house favorite. Try the lamb biryani or one of the many vegetarian dishes. You must order the stuffed naan and garlic naan for the table, using it to mop up the sauce on your plate. More than likely, you'll want boxes all around, which gives you room to order one of the wonderful desserts like mango ice cream or kheer, which is very similar to rice pudding.

8447 Copper Creek Blvd., Bradenton, 941-926-3077
tandoorsarasota.com

17

DINE ON MODERN SEAFOOD AND CREATIVE COCKTAILS AT SHORE

Both locations of Shore in our area are amazing, but with a slightly different vibe. The St. Armands location is hip and fun, with outdoor seating overlooking John Ringling Boulevard. The Longboat Key location has more of a beachy feel and spectacular views of Sarasota Bay. One thing both have in common is fantastic food. We love starting with the Kung Pao calamari and jumbo lump crab cake along with a couple of glasses of wine from their extensive list. The cocktail menu offers creative concoctions like the Pear Old Fashioned or the Blood Orange Margarita. The Key West shrimp and scallop risotto is a popular favorite and the black grouper tacos are exceptional. There's a lot of seafood on the menu, but meat lovers will have great choices, too, like ribs, burgers, or meat loaf. Our suggestion is always to order several different things and share so you can taste everything!

465 John Ringling Blvd., Ste. 200, 941-296 0301
800 Broadway St., Longboat Key, 941-259-4600
dineshore.com

18

EXPERIENCE THE WEIRDEST OLD FLORIDA RESTAURANT

AT LINGER LODGE

The Linger Lodge name kind of gets you, doesn't it? Makes you think of lazy days on the river, eating ribs or burgers served up with coleslaw and baked beans. At Linger Lodge you can also order a plate of frog legs and alligator bites, or add catfish and make it a combo. While you wait for your food to be delivered by a knowledgeable server who by now has told you to read the story of Linger Lodge, you can get up and take a walk around to see some of the animals from the story. All weirdness aside, the food is really good at Linger Lodge. There's a lot to choose from, including all kinds of goodness from their smoker menu. The Shrimp Sizzler entrée and the half-pound Linger Burger were both cooked perfectly, washed down with a local beer. Be sure to take a peek at the Road Kill menu.

7116 85th St. Ct. E, Bradenton, 941-755-2757
lingerlodge.com

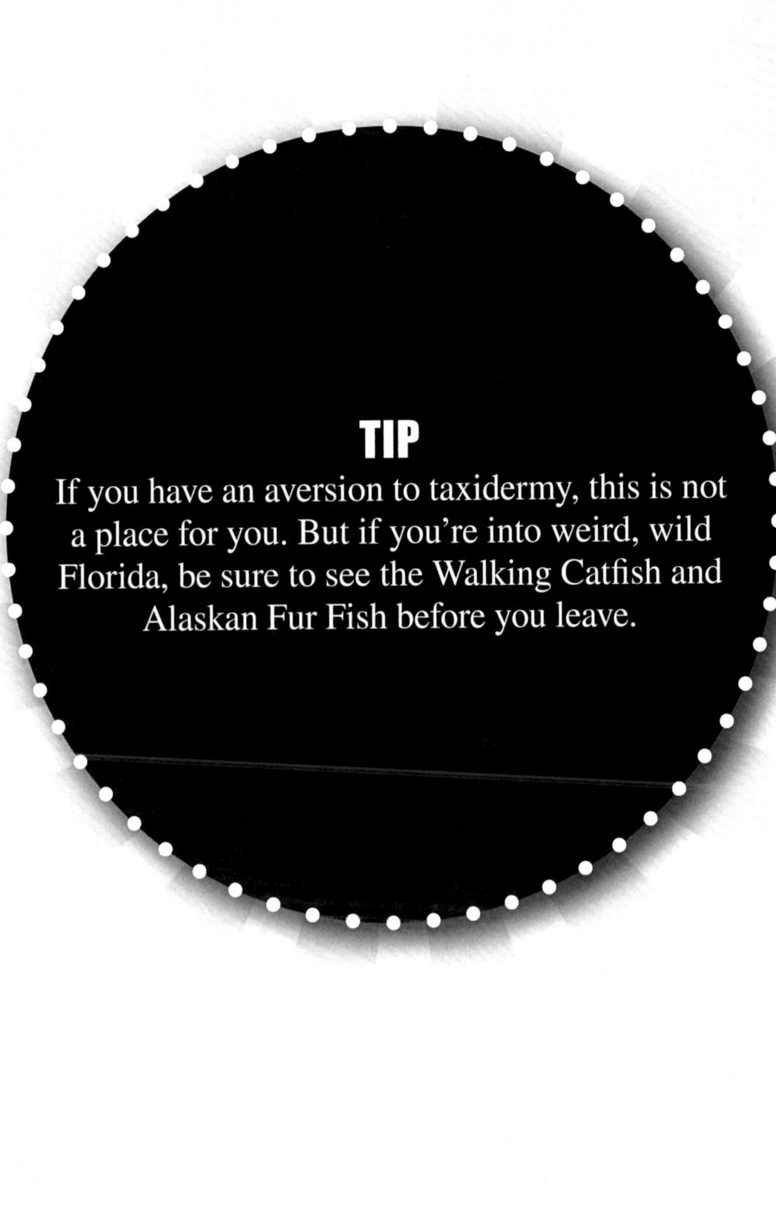
TIP
If you have an aversion to taxidermy, this is not a place for you. But if you're into weird, wild Florida, be sure to see the Walking Catfish and Alaskan Fur Fish before you leave.

19

SIP A LOCAL BEER FLIGHT
AT GOOD LIQUID

The Sarasota-Bradenton area has a handful of breweries, most of which offer food from food trucks. At Good Liquid Brewing Co., the beer and food menus are both long, and it's all delicious. We like trying the latest craft beers, so we usually order a flight, but you can also get four-ounce pours that are perfect for a quick taste while you're out exploring Waterside, a fabulous outdoor venue with more restaurants and shops. On the appetizer menu, try the GLB Pretzel with beer cheese fondue, the perfect pairing with a brew. The tempura cauliflower and Cast Iron Meatballs are fantastic, too. We often order a few appetizers instead of entrées as we like to try different things. For entrées, the burgers are generous portions, always cooked perfectly, and come in several varieties. You can't go wrong with a Brewzetta (pizza) or the black pepper chicken and shrimp. Salads and vegan dishes are available, too.

1570 Lakefront Dr., 941-770-4282
goodliquidbrewingcompany.com

TIP

Good Liquid Distillery & Cocktail Lounge is about a one-minute walk away and serves creative cocktails, crushes, and a create-your-own old-fashioned.

MORE LOCAL BREWERIES

3 Car Garage Brewing Company
8405 Heritage Green Way, Bradenton, 941-741-8877
3cargaragebrewing.com

3 Keys Brewing & Gastrobrew
2505 Manatee Ave E., Bradenton, 941-218-0396
3keysbrewing.com

Big Top Brewing Company
975 Cattlemen Rd., 941-371-2939
2507 Lakewood Ranch Blvd., Bradenton, 941-708-2966
bigtopbrewing.com

Calusa Brewing
5377 McIntosh Rd., 941-552-8846
calusabrewing.com

Motorworks Brewing
1014 9th St. W, Bradenton, 941-567-6218
motorworksbrewing.com

Sun King Brewery
1215 Mango Ave., 941-893-3940
sunkingbrewing.com

SAVOR FRESH SEAFOOD WITH A STUNNING VIEW

AT TIDE TABLES

Tide Tables is another laid-back favorite of the locals. It's located at mile marker 48, and you can arrive by boat or car. There may be a wait, but one of the friendly staff will direct you to tables out on the adjoining pier where you can sip on a cold beverage until your table is ready. This is the last working commercial fishing village on the Gulf Coast of Florida, so you might just see fishermen pulling in a daily catch. Speaking of seafood, it doesn't get fresher than this. Start with the conch fritters or grouper spread. For your main course, we love the grouper sandwich with a side of fries and their delicious homemade coleslaw or baked beans. There's a burger or chicken sandwich for those who don't like seafood. Most of the seating is outdoors overlooking the Intracoastal Waterway. There is inside seating, too, but I've never been able to pull myself away from that view.

12507 Cortez Rd. W, Bradenton, 941-567-6206
tidetablescortez.com

BE AWED
AT MICHAEL JOHN'S

The first time I visited Michael John's, 14 years ago, I couldn't believe our luck to have such an outstanding restaurant so close to home. Somehow, MJ's just keeps getting better. Chef and owner Michael John Auer learned from the best, starting with his mom. Later in life, while pursing his love for cooking, he worked at the Brasserie Le Coze in Atlanta, the restaurant venture with siblings Maguy and Gilbert Le Coze and Eric Ripert. After learning from some of the top chefs in the world, Auer ended up in Bradenton opening Michael John's with a mission statement of "Do it well, do it consistent, and keep it simple." Michael John's was opened as an American brasserie but has "morphed into a steakhouse." One bite of the food, whether a steak, seafood, or one of their decadent desserts, and you won't care what they call it. You'll just want to go back.

1040 Carlton Arms Blvd., Bradenton, 941-747-8032
michaeljohnsrestaurant.com

TIP

Though MJ's is known for fine dining, the bar is perfect for hanging out for a glass of wine or a beer and one of the filet mignon burgers and an order of fries.

TAKE A TRIP TO GREECE THROUGH YOUR TASTE BUDS

AT BLU KOUZINA

At this lovely restaurant located on St. Armands Circle, you can enjoy some of the best Greek food anywhere. Blu Kouzina is one of our favorite spots for appetizers; I'd suggest starting with cold *mezedes*, like the dolmades, commonly known as stuffed grape leaves, and the taramosalata, cod roe dip. Move on to the hot starters and order the keftedes, tender, juicy meatballs with a side of tzatziki, as well as the saganaki with figs—traditional salty white cheese with sweet figs—and finally the spanakopita, a flaky pastry filled with spinach, feta cheese, and herbs. They have a lot of traditional entrées to choose from, too, like the grilled whole fresh fish or moussaka. Order a bottle of one of their wonderful Greek wines to pair with your meal. Finish off with something from the dessert menu. In addition to excellent food, the outdoor seating area is perfect for people-watching and enjoying the beautiful Florida weather.

24 N Blvd. of the Presidents, 941-388-2619
295 N Cattleman Rd., Ste. 4
blukouzina.com/us

CHOW DOWN ON AMAZING MEXICAN FOOD
AT WICKED CANTINA

This is one of our favorite Mexican restaurants. With two locations, you'll have your choice of vibe. The beach location is fun, with plenty of indoor and outdoor seating under umbrellas to block the sun. The Sarasota location has more menu choices, but the food is seriously delicious at both. The cocktails are creative and fun. Try the Sweet Heat margarita, the smoky mezcalita, or one of their frozen concoctions. When it comes to the food, the menu has a lot of options. I like to order a few things and share so I can taste it all. I asked for suggestions and started with the Wicked Roll, Wicked Queso, and an order of their delicious guacamole. The Wicked Queso is out of this world. For our entrées, we chose shrimp tacos, brisket tacos, and carnitas street tacos. The Bradenton Beach location also serves breakfast. Check the live music calendar on the website.

1603 N Tamiami Trl., 941-706-2395
101 7th St. N, Bradenton Beach, 941-281-2990
wickedcantina.com

24

ENJOY FRESH SEAFOOD WITH A VIEW OF THE BEACH

AT FINS AT SHARKY'S

I've eaten at Fins several times, and the food is always superb. There's indoor and outdoor seating, but the view of the beach is pretty spectacular. Watching the beautiful waves of the Gulf of Mexico rolling up on the sand along with the sounds of the surf . . . it doesn't get much better for alfresco dining! Fins uses local ingredients as much as possible, and you'll have to make a trip back as you'll want to try everything. Start with one of their creative cocktails and the oysters Rockefeller. Baked in their Josper oven, they are seasoned perfectly and you can still taste the sea. The North Atlantic cod fish and chips is one of their most popular dishes. The fish was delicate and battered just enough to give it a crunch. We enjoyed the Pacific mahi mahi sandwich and the mahi mahi tacos, too. Fins is known for their steaks and sushi, so I'm headed back soon to try both.

1600 Harbor Dr. S, Venice, 941-999-3467
finsatsharkys.com

FEAST ON RUSTIC ITALIAN
AT TAVERNA TOSCANA

Taverna Toscana offers rustic Italian cuisine in the heart of downtown Bradenton. With celebrity chef Fabio Viviani at the helm, expect to be wowed. Chef Fabio grew up in Florence, Italy, making his way to the United States in 2005 where he opened his first US-based restaurants, all in Los Angeles. Eventually, Chef Fabio found his way to our area, where he opened the upscale Taverna Toscana. The inside of the restaurant is bright and modern, with an expansive bar area. The outdoor patio is huge but cozy. Though the restaurant is considered Italian, don't expect a lot of traditional dishes like lasagna and spaghetti. Instead, you'll find entrées like roasted seabass, wagyu short rib bolognese, and butcher cut steaks. Don't miss the appetizer menu. The crostini del giorno, grilled bone marrow, and Fabio's wagyu meatball are all heavenly. Pair your meal with one of their creative craft cocktails, or choose a wine from their long list.

1301 6th Ave W, Bradenton, 941-357-7772
tavernatoscana.com

DINE INSIDE ONE OF SARASOTA'S MOST HISTORIC LANDMARKS

AT SAGE SRQ

An eclectic dining experience awaits inside the historic Sarasota Times Building, one of the city's most famous landmarks. Built in 1925 and added to the National Register of Historic Places in 1984, this building was designed by American architect Dwight James Baum, whose work includes Cá d'Zan—John and Mable Ringling's mansion—as well as the historic Sarasota Courthouse. Once inside, you'll have choices of seating and accompanying vibe. The main dining room is spacious with high ceilings. The second floor is more intimate. Sage Rooftop is fun and offers a 360-degree view of downtown. Finally, the first-floor bar is great for a casual meal. The menu is creative with starters like the apple-pear-prosciutto stack or pan seared foie gras. For an entrée, try the black cod in ginger-mirin-soy glaze or the shredded lamb shank with red wine reduction. Your server will happily help you choose a wine to pair with your meal. Don't leave without at least taking a look at the dessert menu.

1216 1st St., 941-445-5660
sagesrq.com

HAVE ONE, TWO, BUT NOT THREE

AT BAHI HUT TIKI COCKTAIL LOUNGE

Bahi Hut has been serving up their famous mai tai since 1954. One sip and you'll know why there's a limit of two per person! This recipe has been handed down to the current owners from the previous owners and the owners before them, dating back 68 years. If a mai tai isn't your thing, you might want to try their very own Bahi Aloha, made with two varieties of the area's own Siesta Key Rum. This is a great spot to chill out after exploring the area. The whimsical decor is fun and inviting. Live entertainment starts at 7 p.m. on Fridays and Saturdays. Drag Queen Bingo is on Sunday night, so you can mark that off your bucket list! For a real treat, book a room at the 1950s-inspired Golden Host Resort and be just steps from your retro-style room. Maybe they allow a third mai tai if you're staying there?

4675 N Tamiami Trl., 941-355-5141
bahihut.com

TIP

Bahi Hut has snacks but does not serve meals, so eat before you go.

EXPERIENCE FINE DINING
AT MICHAEL'S ON EAST

One of the most iconic restaurants in Sarasota, Michael's on East received their 34th consecutive AAA Four-Diamond Award as well as Best of Award Excellence for its wine program by *Wine Spectator* in 2023. Michael's is known for its upscale food and wines from around the world; dining here is not just eating out, but an experience. With a 1940s supper club vibe, this is the perfect place for a romantic dinner, though you'll see groups of friends dining together, too. The menu has a plethora of seafood, as it should on the Gulf Coast of Florida, but you'll also see steaks, rack of lamb, and duck. Choose from starters like Key West shrimp Mozambique or Maine lobster bisque. For your entrée, try the East Avenue bouillabaisse, scallop & shrimp butternut squash ravioli, or the USDA Prime New York strip. Ask your server to suggest a wine pairing. Save room for one of their amazing desserts!

1212 East Ave. S, 941-366-0007
bestfood.com

Michael's on East hosts monthly wine dinners and wine tastings, and even puts together exclusive trips to top wine destinations. Ask while you're there or visit the website for more information. Selected by Open Table as one of the Top 100 Romantic Restaurants in America for 2024, this is the spot for an anniversary or date night!

Circus Sarasota

MUSIC
AND ENTERTAINMENT

29

SEE A BROADWAY-STYLE SHOW
AT ASOLO REP

Where else can you see a show at a theater built in Italy in 1798 and reassembled in Sarasota? The interior of this 18th-century theater in Asolo, Italy, was spotted by the first director of the John and Mable Ringling Museum of Art and purchased in 1949 for the museum's collection. This was the beginning of the Asolo Theatre Festival and later the Asolo Theater Company. Audiences outgrew the theater, which moved to its home at Florida State University Center for the Performing Arts. The Asolo Repertory Theatre is the largest professional theater in the entire state of Florida and the Southeastern United States. Asolo celebrated its 65th anniversary in 2024. The actors include Broadway and regional talent. All the sets and costumes you'll see in performances were made locally in Sarasota. Past performances include *The Three Musketeers*, *Hair*, *Evita*, and *Twelve Angry Men*. In addition to a full calendar of shows, Asolo also offers young artist camps and classes, adult classes, and more.

5555 N Tamiami Trl., 941-351-8000
asolorep.org

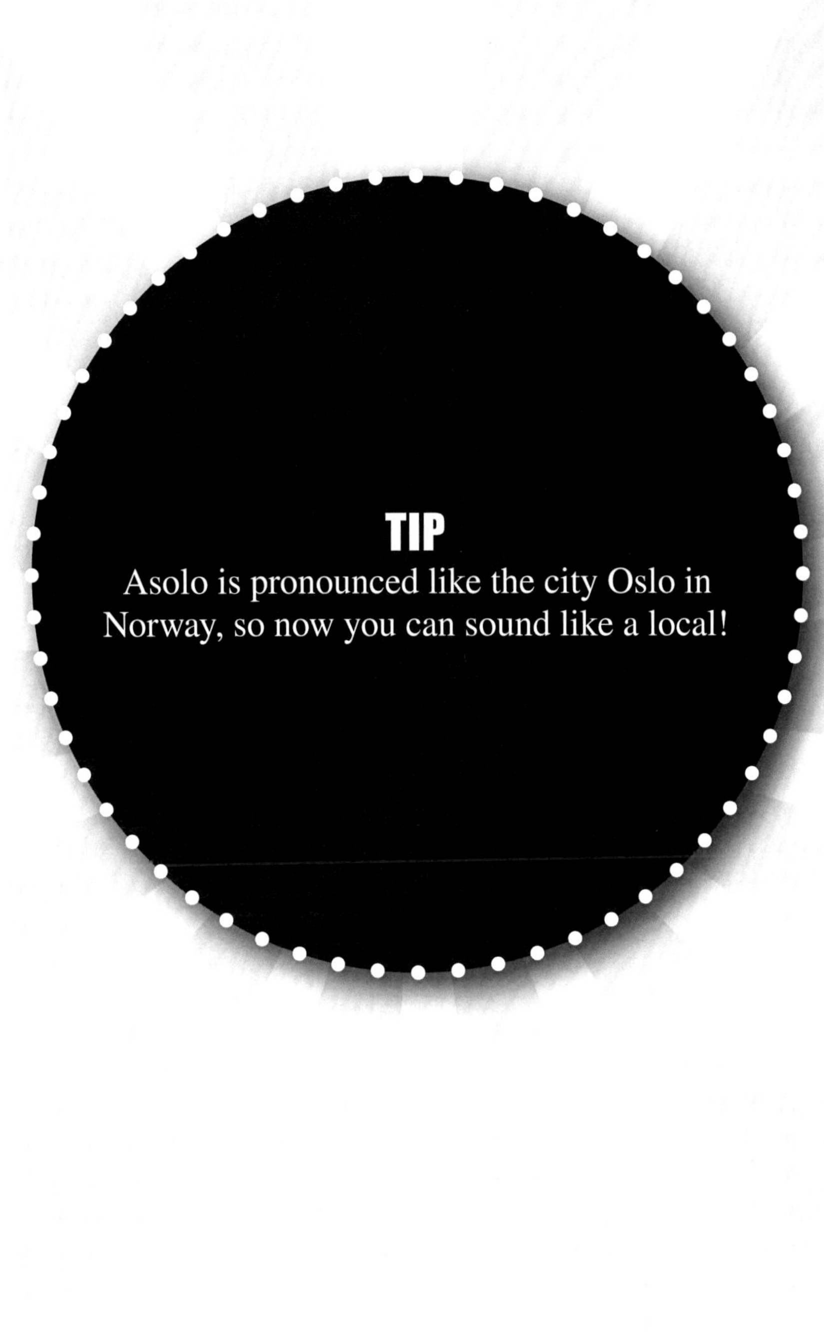
TIP
Asolo is pronounced like the city Oslo in Norway, so now you can sound like a local!

30

BE MOVED
BY A SARASOTA OPERA PERFORMANCE

One of the true gems of Sarasota, the Sarasota Opera House has quite a history. Originally commissioned to architect Roy A. Benjamin by A.B. Edwards, first mayor of Sarasota, this multipurpose building was unveiled in April 1926. Many popular performers took the stage at the A.B. Edwards Theater, including Will Rogers, the Ziegfeld Follies, and in 1956, Elvis Presley. Through the years the building deteriorated, closing in 1973. All the while, the touring opera group, which would become the Asolo Opera Company, had been sharing the Historic Asolo Theatre during the winter and was hoping for their own opera house to support their growing audience. The company moved to the historic Edwards Theater in 1984, changing their name to Sarasota Opera, and the newly named Sarasota Opera House opened with its first production that year. Additional renovations have taken place to create a theater referred to by *Musical America* as one of the finest venues for opera in the United States.

61 N Pineapple Ave., 941-328-1300
sarasotaopera.org

TIP

See a performance of the Sarasota Youth Opera, or better yet, get your children involved. It is a wonderful youth program!

31

SEE A SHOW
AT VAN WEZEL HALL

Welcome to the world's only purple shell-shaped theater. Designed by architect William Wesley Peters, son-in-law of Frank Lloyd Wright, this unique hall was built with money from the city of Sarasota and an endowment from local philanthropists Lewis and Eugenia Van Wezel.

Van Wezel Hall typically hosts over 100 performances per season, from top national and international performers to Broadway musicals to symphonies to comedians and more. In addition, you can also see performances here from the Sarasota Ballet and Sarasota Orchestra, as well as the Sarasota Concert Association. Past performances have included Duke Ellington, Tony Bennett, B.B. King, Dolly Parton, and John Legend. See the calendar for upcoming performances. Note: Some of the top shows are only available to season ticket holders, which is a great way to commit to date night at least three times per year. You know who you are. And by the way, it's pronounced Van Wayzull. You're welcome.

777 N Tamiami Trl., 941-263-6799
vanwezel.org

32

LAUGH UNTIL YOU CRY
AT MCCURDY'S COMEDY THEATRE

If you're looking for a good laugh (and who isn't these days?), McCurdy's Comedy Theatre and Humor Institute is the spot. Dedicated to stand-up comedy, this 4,200-square-foot showroom with cabaret-style seating is located in the heart of Sarasota. McCurdy's features mostly one-man shows, but special events include Open Bar Comedy with three powerhouse headliners, Drag Queen Bingo, and Hard Heart Burlesque. Check out Humor Institute's Class Performance Night or get up on the stage yourself for Open Mic Night on Thursdays. Don't think you're funny enough? Why not sign up for the popular Stand-Up Comedy Boot Camp? McCurdy's also has holiday events, so check out the calendar and pick a show you'd like to see. Start your evening in the Green Room for a cocktail or bite to eat before the show. The menu features appetizers, bigger bites like a caprese flatbread and burgers, and several desserts.

1923 Ringling Blvd., 941-925-3869
mccurdyscomedy.com

33

BE THRILLED
AT A LIVE CIRCUS PERFORMANCE

With Sarasota's long history with the Ringling Bros. and Barnum & Bailey Circus, The Circus Arts Conservancy aims to keep live performances going by not only hosting circus shows but also featuring special events throughout the year. This means you'll be able to see Sarasota Circus performances, as well as shows from Sailor Circus, called *The Greatest Little Show On Earth*, and the longest-running youth circus in the United States. Shows take place at different venues around the Sarasota area. In addition, a collaboration with Nik Wallenda, international high-wire celebrity and Sarasota's local hometown hero, will bring holiday spectaculars to our area where Wallenda will also perform. Have a daring child age 8–18 with circus-worthy talent? Check out the Sailor Circus Academy, a training program just for students in Sarasota and Manatee Counties. 60 to 90 minute recreational classes for adults are also available for flying trapeze, aerial silks, trampoline, lyra (hoops), and more. Check out the youth camps, too.

2075 Bahia Vista St., 941-355-9335
circusarts.org

EXPERIENCE
AN AUTHENTIC DRUM CIRCLE

About an hour before the sun sets on Sundays, the rhythm begins. Since 1996, families and friends have been meeting for the drum circle in the sand right on Siesta Beach. Look for the crowd with drums. It may seem awkward at first if you've never experienced anything like a drum circle, but go with the flow as you'll probably never have the chance to experience anything like it again, at least until your next visit to Siesta Key. I've traveled to 40 countries on five continents, but I've never seen anything like this drum circle. Once the beat starts, the dancing begins, too. Some of the musicians and dancers come every week; others were spectators the week before and came back with a drum. Somehow, it always works. Join in on the fun of this celebration of sundown. Parking is available near the circle. There's a playground and a concession stand.

Siesta Key Beach, 948 Beach Rd., Siesta Key
siestakeychamber.com/drum-circle

ATTEND AWARD-WINNING COMMUNITY PERFORMANCES

AT VENICE THEATRE

The first show at Venice Theatre was over 70 years ago. It was called Venice Little Theater at that time; the show took place in a borrowed building, with an all-volunteer staff, and got by on $2 admission tickets. Today, this award-winning theater is the largest community theater, per capita, in the United States and operates on a budget of about $4 million. Even after the devastating setback of Hurricane Ian, the Venice Theatre is rebuilding with plans to be better than ever. With musical tributes to acts like Elvis Presley, Barbra Streisand, and Aretha Franklin and classic musicals like *Gypsy* and *The Spitfire Grill*, this theater brings our area fabulous entertainment at affordable prices with not a bad seat in the house. In addition, the Venice Theatre has classes for children in elementary through high school, a summer stock program for high school and college students pursuing a career in theater and adult theater training classes.

140 Tampa Ave. W, Venice, 941-488-1115
venicetheatre.org

36

LISTEN TO THE OLDEST CONTINUOUSLY OPERATING ORCHESTRA IN THE STATE

AT SARASOTA ORCHESTRA

Sarasota Orchestra has been entertaining music lovers since 1949, performing over 100 concerts every year. In fact, it's the oldest continuously operating orchestra in the state. Every year, the 76-member orchestra performs more than 100 concerts spread across classical, pops, chamber music, and community outreach shows. Concerts are held at a variety of venues, including the Van Wezel, Holley Hall, and Sarasota Opera House. Tickets may be purchased online, but you can also often snag a ticket right at the box office just prior to the concert, so don't think you can't attend if you just happen to be in town! Unless it's a sold-out performance, tickets will be available beginning one hour before showtime. Sarasota Orchestra also works with local schools to introduce youth to the orchestra through their Young Person's Concerts, Summer Music Camp, and Youth Orchestra. If you've never been to an orchestra, you're in for a thrill!

709 N Tamiami Trl., 941-953-3434
sarasotaorchestra.org

GO TO THE MOVIES
AT THE SARASOTA FILM SOCIETY

The nonprofit, member-supported Sarasota Film Society was founded in 1984, bringing first-run, independent, foreign-language, and art-related films to the Sarasota-Bradenton area. The Society consists of two theaters: the classic Burns Court Theater and the newer Lakewood Ranch Cinema. Both theaters show blockbuster hits as well as hosting special events like screenings with a question-and-answer panel after the film and special film-related costume contests. Every November, the Sarasota Film Society at Burns Court hosts the Cineworld Film Festival, one of the oldest film festivals in the state of Florida, as well as an annual Oscars viewing party in late February or early March. Military personnel and their families can attend Movies for Heroes at the Lakewood Ranch location. Check the calendar for showtimes and to see what's playing. Both theaters have concessions with food and drink. Both are also within walking distance of restaurants and shopping, so make a night of it!

506 Burns Ln., 941-955-3456
10715 Rodeo Dr., Ste. 8, Lakewood Ranch, 941-955-3456
filmsociety.org

38

TAKE IN A DANCE PERFORMANCE

AT SARASOTA BALLET

Though Florida's population has been booming, the state only has one professional ballet company, and we're incredibly lucky to have it right here in Sarasota. Founded in 1987, the Sarasota Ballet has received praise from the *Wall Street Journal*, the *Washington Post*, and the *New York Times*, just to name a few. The company has been invited to perform at the Kennedy Center in Washington, DC, the Joyce Center in New York City, and other prestigious venues. If you haven't experienced a performance of the Sarasota Ballet, take a look at the upcoming season overview. The shows take place at our beautiful Sarasota Opera House, the FSU Center for the Performing Arts, and the Van Wezel Performing Arts Hall. In addition to performances, the Sarasota Ballet hosts a plethora of community programs such as Experience Days for children ages 3 and up, school and adult programs, and even a class for those with Parkinson's.

5555 N Tamiami Trl., 941-359-0099
sarasotaballet.org

Sometimes the front row is not better. I sat in the front and could not see the feet of the dancers at all. Grab seats about halfway back or even farther if you want to sit in orchestra seating. This venue is small, so you'll be able to see everything from just about everywhere . . . except the front few rows.

BE INSPIRED
AT THE VENICE SYMPHONY

The Venice Symphony was one of my favorite discoveries while writing this book. Who knew world-class entertainers performed at this small-town venue? The symphony was incorporated in November of 1974, so 2024 marks its 50th anniversary. What began with a group of volunteers consisting of students and semiprofessional musicians has become a fully professional 75-piece orchestra. With classical music, pops, folk, and even music from films, there really is something for everyone. The Venice Symphony even has a summer music camp and youth orchestra program. Troy Quinn, conductor of the Venice Symphony, says everyone loves symphonic music; they just don't know it yet if they haven't been to the symphony. Past performances include the Movie Maestro: A Tribute to John Williams; A Night at the Museum; the always popular Holiday Spectacular; and Hooray for Hollywood with Michael Feinstein, which was incredible! The Symphony performances often sell out, so keep an eye on their website and get your tickets early.

700 US 41 Bypass N, Ste. 4, Venice, 941-207-8822
thevenicesymphony.org

WATCH A MOVIE UNDER THE STARS
AT RUSKIN FAMILY DRIVE-IN

According to data collected from driveinmovie.com, there are only around 300 drive-ins left in the US, down from over 4,000 in the 1950s. In our state, as of this writing, we have 10, and the Ruskin Family Drive-In Theatre is the closest to our area. The drive is 35 minutes from Bradenton and is a great family-friendly activity. There's nothing like seeing a movie under the stars. Ruskin Family Drive-In showed their first movie, *Singin' in the Rain*, in 1952, and they have been a community gathering place ever since. The drive-in has clean restrooms and a designated area for the kids to play. With a 2,000-square-foot screen, you will see a movie like never before.

The concession stand has more choices than your typical drive-in, offering homemade pizza, hot dogs with toppings, chili, nachos, ice cream, candy, and of course, popcorn! Note: The Ruskin Family Drive-In Theatre is cash only. No credit cards accepted.

5011 US Hwy 41 N, Ruskin, 813-645-1455
ruskinfamilydrivein.com

Kayaks at Anna Maria Island

SPORTS AND RECREATION

SEE THE BAY
BY KAYAK

Pick a Saturday to take a free two-hour guided kayak tour at 8:30 a.m. to see the restored mangroves of Sarasota Bay. Mangroves are part of Florida's state heritage, with about 600,000 acres of mangrove forests statewide. Sarasota Bay offers one of the best experiences to explore these true Florida natives. You never know what you might see, from manatees, bottlenose dolphins, and fish to a large variety of birds such as great blue herons, osprey, and roseate spoonbills. This is an intermediate-level tour with Ride & Paddle's experienced guides, so it's best if you have kayaked before. Kids must be 12 or older and accompanied by a parent or guardian. Kayaks and life jackets are included. The group meets at the Bay Park's ADA-accessible kayak launch site. Note: You must register in advance to be sure there will be a kayak for you and the rest of your party.

655 N Tamiami Trl., 941-203-5316
thebaysarasota.org/event/ride-paddle-guided-kayak-tour

TIP

If you're looking for a smaller or private guided tour, the Sarasota-Bradenton area has a plethora of guided tour companies. Experienced kayakers might prefer to simply rent kayaks and explore on their own.

TAKE A WALK
THROUGH CELERY FIELDS

Just about 100 years ago, an experimental farm was constructed in this spot. Because the land was rich in peat, it was thought to be good for growing vegetables. After trying different varieties, it was decided in 1927 that celery would be the predominant crop in these low-lying, damp fields. In fact, celery was still grown there until Sarasota County purchased it in 1995. Today, you'll find two boardwalks perfect for walking, biking, and wildlife viewing. Keep your eyes open for one of the 246 bird species found here, such as the limpkin, barn owl, and eastern meadowlark. Even rare birds for the Sarasota area like the white-rumped sandpiper have been spotted, making Celery Fields one of the most popular spots on the Great Florida Birding Trail. What's more, there has been confirmation of early native settlement with paleontological artifacts found. Stop by the Nature Center to learn more from the Sarasota Audubon docents, who are always eager to answer your questions.

999 Center Rd., 941-312-6533
sarasotaaudubon.org/the-celery-fields

GET YOUR STEPS IN
ON THE JOHN RINGLING BRIDGE WALK

Connecting Sarasota and St. Armands Circle, the John Ringling Bridge spans the Sarasota Bay, 65 feet in the air. Whether you walk, jog, or bike across the John Ringling Causeway, you'll be treated to views of the beautiful bay and towers of downtown Sarasota. Named after John Ringling, who financed the building of the first bridge in 1925 connecting the islands with the mainland, the bridge was rebuilt to a four-lane drawbridge in the 1950s as the city's traffic grew. It didn't take long for the traffic to outgrow the bridge again, and it was rebuilt once more in the early 2000s, opening in 2003. If you start at Bird Key Park and walk until the bridge ends and back again, it's a little over two miles. For a longer walk, you can head to St. Armands Circle and back, which is about five miles total. Wear sunscreen and a hat, and bring a bottle of water.

2 Marina Plaza

TIP

You may get lucky and find a free parking spot, but garage parking is plentiful.

MEET A MANATEE
AT MOTE MARINE AQUARIUM

Buffet the manatee is a long-time resident of Mote Marine Aquarium. His job is to introduce visitors to the manatee so they can learn about ways to protect his friends in the wild. Join him for lunch each day around noon and see just how much these gentle giants can eat! After you say hello to Buffet, explore the rest of this amazing aquarium, where you can learn about playful otters, sea turtles, stingrays, and even sharks! In Mote's Virtual Reality Experience, choose from one of five experiences, like swimming with a humpback whale and her calf and diving in search of some of the world's largest sharks. Mote has a calendar full of special events like Breakfast with the Sharks, Deep Netting in the Bay, science talks, and summer camps. Reserve early, as many of these events sell out. Mote is also known for providing wonderful scout and homeschool programming.

1600 Ken Thompson Pkwy., 941-388-4441
mote.org

45

GO WILD
AT SARASOTA JUNGLE GARDENS

Wildlife fans of all ages will delight in this 10-acre habitat housing more than 200 native and exotic animals. From parrots and porcupines to loveable lemurs, there's a lot to see at Sarasota Jungle Gardens. Twenty-minute shows take place throughout the day where guests can be educated about, and entertained by, residents of this attraction. Get up close at the petting zoo. Step inside the area's first interactive butterfly house. Take a wild walk through the jungle trails. Hand-feed a flamingo from the free roaming flock. Have your photo taken with an alligator. There's so much to do, you might want to spend the whole day. Grab lunch at the Flamingo Cafe. Stop by the gift shop on your way out to pick up a memento, or just take those memories with you. Plus all those photos you took! You'll be talking about this day for years.

3701 Bay Shore Rd., 941-355-5305
sarasotajunglegardens.com

46

TAKE A STROLL
ON THE BRADENTON RIVERWALK

Bradenton's Riverwalk is a project of Realize Bradenton, with a goal of presenting downtown Bradenton as a beautiful, vibrant, and healthy community. Take a stroll along the one-and-a-half-mile public walkway and see the action at the skate park or join in a beach volleyball game. Looking to chill? Relax on one of the permanent loungers and take in the view of the Manatee River. You might even see a boat pull into one of the marinas with its catch of the day. You'll also find The Bishop Museum of Science and Nature just steps away from the Riverwalk. When it's time to eat, there's a vibrant restaurant scene with some of the freshest seafood around, whether on the river or on Old Main Street. This is a fantastic spot to see one of the gorgeous sunsets the Gulf Coast is so proud of.

452 3rd Ave. W, Bradenton, 941-932-9400
cityofbradenton.com/parksrec

TIP

Sunset is a busy time near the water, so if you're planning to go to one of the restaurants with a view, make sure to either make a reservation or get there early.

47

SIFT THE SAND FOR SHARK TEETH

AT CASPERSEN BEACH

Venice, Florida, is the shark's tooth capital of the world, so you will more than likely come home with at least one shark's tooth, which could very well be prehistoric! After all, the waters of this area were chock-full of sharks 10 million years ago when Florida was underwater. The sharks from that period left skeletons, which have disintegrated, and teeth, which remain. This is the spot where nature lovers as well as shark enthusiasts come to find the teeth of the prehistoric sharks as well as the 15 separate species of sharks that currently live in the Sunshine State. In 2023, a charter boat captain found a megalodon shark tooth measuring 6.25 inches off the coast of Sarasota. Ready to go shark-tooth hunting? Head to Caspersen Beach, Casey Key, or Manasota Key. For best results, pick up a Venice Snow Shovel, available at Papa's Bait Shop on Venice Pier.

4100 Harbor Dr. S, Venice
visitvenicefl.org/places/caspersen-beach

48

WATCH WORLD-CLASS ROWING

AT NATHAN BENDERSON PARK

Once a borrow pit where earth was taken for projects elsewhere, Nathan Benderson Park is now a world-class rowing venue hosting events all year long. Past events include the US Olympic & Paralympic Rowing Team Trials, USRowing Winter Speed Order, and the American Youth Cup Regatta. Though rowing is clearly the most popular sport event held at this park, other important aquatic sporting events have been held there, too, such as open-water swimming and stand-up paddleboarding, including the 2024 ICF SUP World Championship. If you'd rather get some exercise yourself instead of being a spectator, Nathan Benderson Park has a 3.4-mile paved trail around the lake, perfect for getting some fresh air with your family or furry friend. You'll more than likely encounter other walkers, bikers, and even a skater or two. There's also a playground for the kids. Check the website for special events, like charity walks and seasonal celebrations.

5851 Nathan Benderson Cir., 941-358-7275
nathanbendersonpark.org

49

TAKE A HIKE
AT NEAL PRESERVE

Neal Preserve is a 120-acre preserve featuring a few opportunities for recreation, including a short shell trail loop, winding boardwalks, and a 20-foot-tall observation tower providing views across the bay. History lovers will be thrilled to wind their way past the reconstructed sacred burial mounds and areas where Native Americans lived from 3000 BC to AD 1400. The Smithsonian excavated the original burial mounds in the 1930s. Neal Preserve is another great spot for birding. In fact, because many of the birds nest here, bikes are not allowed on the trails and pets are not allowed at all. Though this preserve is smaller in comparison to others in the area, it's really one of the most beautiful, and it's easy to access from Manatee Avenue just before the bridge to Anna Maria Island. This is a great family activity for all ages, as it won't take long to see it all.

12301 Manatee Ave. W, Bradenton, 941-748-4501
mymanatee.org/departments/natural_resources/preserves/neal

MORE LOCAL PRESERVES AND STATE PARKS TO EXPLORE

Myakka River State Park
Top feature: 25-foot-high canopy walkway with 74-foot-high tower for nature viewing
13208 State Rd. 72, 941-361-6511
floridastateparks.org/parks-and-trails/myakka-river-state-park

Red Bug Slough Preserve
Top feature: Birding
5200 Beneva Rd., 941-861-5000
visitsarasota.com/beaches-parks/red-bug-slough-preserve

Emerson Point Preserve
Top feature: Historic remains of ancient civilization, observation tower
5801 17th St. W, Palmetto
mymanatee.org/departments/natural_resources/preserves/emerson

Leffis Key Preserve
Top feature: 26-foot-high hill with a 360-degree view of Sarasota Bay and the Gulf of Mexico
2351 Gulf Dr. S, Anna Maria Island
mymanatee.org/departments/natural_resources/preserves/leffis

Robinson Preserve
Top feature: NEST and Canopy Zone
10299 9th Ave. NW, Bradenton
mymanatee.org/departments/natural_resources/preserves/robinson

Rye Preserve
Top feature: Wildlife viewing areas, home to rare gopher tortoise and Florida scrub jay
905 Rye Wilderness Trl., Parrish
mymanatee.org/departments/natural_resources/preserves/rye

RIDE A HORSE ON THE BEACH

AT PALMA SOLA BAY WITH C PONIES

Who hasn't dreamed of riding a horse on a beach? With C Ponies, you can actually get in the water on your horse for the most unforgettable experience! Carmen Herrmann Hanson, owner of C Ponies, is the granddaughter of Colonel Ottomar Herrmann from Herrmann's Royal Lipizzans. With a background like that, it's no wonder Carmen has such a love for horses. She has a riding academy and uses horseback swimming to keep her horses cool and exercised in the hot Florida summers. Ninety percent of the ponies have experienced abuse and neglect from previous owners, so being able to give these horses love is important to Carmen. And the horses love the water! Choose from three different rides, including their most popular, the Sunset Ride. C Ponies offers trail rides, too. All rides are one hour and 30 minutes. You won't want to forget this experience, so C Ponies has a photo package to preserve those memories. Book as far in advance as you can!

8400 Manatee Ave. W, Bradenton, 941-773-5196
cponies.com

51

GET OUTSIDE AND PLAY
AT THE BAY

A public park on the Sarasota Bay, this 53-acre park provides a sustainable gathering place to relax, restore, and recharge. You'll find spots perfect for reading or watching the sun set and walking trails with unforgettable views. The Reading Room is a quiet, shaded area, and even has one of the on-site lending libraries close by. The Ibis Playground is where to head with the kids, with a shade-covered pavilion close by for picnic lunches. And speaking of lunch, the Nest is home to the concessions at the park. Pick up sandwiches, salads, or a rice bowl along with a beverage of choice, including beer, wine, and cocktails. The Oval is the spot for outdoor fitness classes as well as concerts and movie screenings. As this park was meant to be accessible for all, it's equipped with an ADA-accessible kayak launch as well as the accessible Mangrove Bayou Walkway, which is 10 feet wide and cushioned.

655 N Tamiami Trl., 941-203-5316
thebaysarasota.org

TIP

Check the schedule of events for free guided kayak tours, fitness classes, outdoor movies, and more.

WATCH
A MAJOR LEAGUE BASEBALL SPRING TRAINING GAME

Sports fans will be thrilled to learn that the Sarasota-Bradenton area is the home-away-from-home spring-training spot for two Major League Baseball teams!

The Baltimore Orioles play at the 8,000-seat Ed Smith Stadium in Sarasota. The excitement begins the minute you walk through the entranceway behind home plate, and see the view of the entire field. This is a great place to watch a game, with many of the same amenities as a major-league ballpark. The Orioles Team Store is the perfect spot to cool off in the air-conditioning while you pick up your authentic Baltimore Orioles gear.

The Pittsburgh Pirates take the field at the 8,500-seat LECOM Park in Bradenton. This ballpark has a boardwalk that spans the outfield where fans can watch pitchers and catchers in the bullpens. LECOM turned 100 in 2023 and is the oldest stadium still used for spring training in the Grapefruit League. The stadium is also home to the Pittsburgh Pirates' High-A minor league team, the Bradenton Marauders.

Ed Smith Stadium
2700 12th St., 941-893-6300
floridagrapefruitleague.com/teams/baltimore-orioles

LECOM Park
1611 9th St. W, Bradenton, 941-747-3031
floridagrapefruitleague.com/teams/pittsburgh-pirates

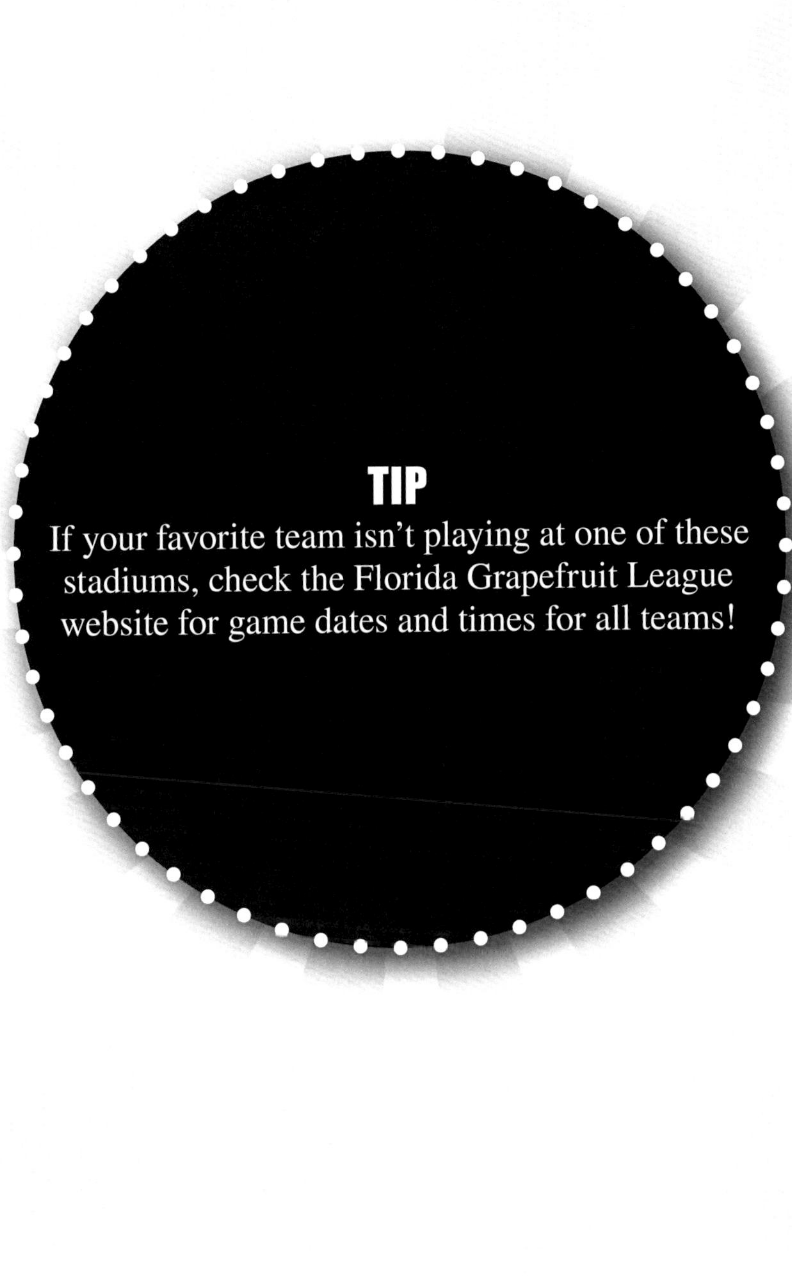

TIP

If your favorite team isn't playing at one of these stadiums, check the Florida Grapefruit League website for game dates and times for all teams!

53

GO FISH
FROM ROD & REEL PIER

Pier fishing is a popular pastime in the area, and you can come home with a bounty if you pick the right spot. Red fish, snook, pompano, and even sharks have been caught from a pier. Most piers offer rentals of rods as well as bait. With easy access to piers, this is a great way to spend an afternoon, even for beginners. Hanging out on a pier under the blue skies with an abundance of seabirds, with a possibility of seeing dolphins and manatees, is not a bad way to spend the day, even if you come home empty handed. Pier fishing is also an inexpensive way to spend the afternoon, with the average rod rental at around $10 for the entire day. Add bait and you're still at less than $15 for a day of fun in the sun, with a good chance that you'll go home with dinner.

875 N Shore Dr., Anna Maria, 941-778-1885
rodreelpier.com

TIP

Be sure to grab a bite to eat as their grouper sandwich is one of the best!

MORE POPULAR LOCATIONS FOR PIER FISHING

Note: Keep in mind that ages 16 to 64 need a fishing license.

Anna Maria Historic City Pier
Bait shop, restaurant, and restrooms
100 S Bay Blvd., Anna Maria
bradentongulfislands.com/listing/anna-maria-city-pier

Bridge Street Pier
Bait shop, restaurant, and restrooms
200 Bridge St., Bradenton Beach

Ken Thompson Park
Restrooms, restaurant, and bait shop nearby
1700 Ken Thompson Pkwy.

Nora Patterson Bay Island Park
Restroom, picnic tables
946 Siesta Dr.

Palma Sola Fishing Pier
Restrooms, picnic tables
9450 Manatee Ave. W, Bradenton

Saprito Fishing Pier
Bait shop and restrooms nearby
920 John Ringling Cswy.

Venice Fishing Pier
Bait shop on pier, restaurant and restrooms nearby
Note: No fishing license required
1600 S Harbor Dr., Venice
venicegov.com/visiting/fishing-pier

Whitaker Gateway Park Fishing Pier
Restrooms
1455 N Tamiami Trl.

bradentongulfislands.com/pages/260/fishing-bradenton-area-waters

54

GET SOME VITAMIN SEA

AT SIESTA BEACH

A visit to the Sarasota-Bradenton area is not complete without at least one beach day, and we have so many incredible beaches to choose from! It's well known that the sand at the beaches of Siesta Key is 99 percent quartz, giving it that beautiful shade of white and preventing it from getting hot and burning your feet. Dr. Beach has named Siesta Beach the #1 beach in the United States twice, and in 2023 TripAdvisor named Siesta Beach #2 in the country and #14 in the world! In 2024, Siesta Beach was named the #1 beach in Florida by *US News & World Report*. You'll find ample parking, a concession stand, and restrooms at this public beach. So grab your bathing suit, towel, flip-flops, sunscreen, cooler for water and snacks, and a good book, and head out to Siesta Beach for the perfect day in the sun!

948 Beach Rd., Siesta Key
siestakeychamber.com/explore-the-key/our-beaches/siesta-beach

TIP

Be on the lookout for parking meters. If you park without paying where a meter is used, you will probably be ticketed.

MORE BEACHES IN THE AREA

Anna Maria Beach
Follow streets on the west side of Anna Maria to the end.
bradentongulfislands.com/listing/anna-maria-beach

Bean Point
Note: Swimming is not recommended because of strong currents.
793 N Shore Dr., Anna Maria
bradentongulfislands.com/listing/bean-point

Caspersen Beach
4100 Harbor Dr., Venice, 941-861-5000
visitsarasota.com/beaches-parks/caspersen-beach

Coquina Beach
Gulf Dr. S, Bradenton Beach
bradentongulfislands.com/discover/beaches

Cortez Beach
698 Gulf Dr. S, Bradenton Beach
bradentongulfislands.com/discover/beaches

Holmes Beach
6317 Gulf Dr., Holmes Beach
bradentongulfislands.com/listing/holmes-beach

Lido Beach
400 Ben Franklin Dr., Lido Key, 941-365-2200
visitsarasota.com/beaches-parks/lido-beach

Manatee Beach
4000 Gulf Dr., Holmes Beach, 941-742-5923
bradentongulfislands.com/listing/manatee-beach

Nokomis Beach
100 Casey Key Rd., Nokomis, 941-861-5000
visitsarasota.com/beaches-parks/nokomis-beach

Turtle Beach
8918 Midnight Pass Rd., 941-861-5000
visitsarasota.com/beaches-parks/turtle-beach

55

PLAY IN THE TREES
AT TREEUMPH!

Ready for an exhilarating adventure? How about climbing and swinging through the trees at this elevated adventure park? TreeUmph! Adventure Course has all kinds of adventure challenges, and what could be better than some good old-fashioned exercise that will keep you smiling throughout the day? What's more, studies show physical challenges give your mind a boost. Take your workout outside in this 14-acre park and zip line, walk the suspension bridge, or try out the floating logs or climbing walls. Get outside and test your skills! Your ticket is good for three hours of adventure, and with 120 games, you'll want to come back for more. There's even a children's ticket for ages 5–8 where parents can climb around with the kids, and annual passes for those who can't get enough. Get your family and friends together for a group trip. Makes a great birthday party venue or gift!

21805 E SR 70, Bradenton, 941-322-2130
treeumph.com/bradenton

TAKE A YOGA CLASS ON THE BEACH

WITH SALTY BUDDHA

If a yoga class on the beach has been on your bucket list, we're happy to help you check it off! Take a Rise & Flow beach yoga class, which is offered for all levels of experience. The intention of Salty Buddha is to help you connect to nature and start your day with healthy movement. Not a morning person? They also offer Sunset Beach Yoga, offering complete relaxation as you move to the sound of the waves, or Full Moon Beach Yoga, honoring solar and lunar energies. The teacher is able to help beginners with modifications. They really want to be accessible for all. You'll need to bring a towel or blanket. Salty Buddha offers their yoga classes on the beach, on paddleboards, and in their Bradenton Beach studio. They also offer Guided Paddle and Floating Meditation. If you've been thinking about getting your zen on, this one's for you!

119 Bridge St., Ste. 230, Bradenton, 941-209-8848
saltybuddhaco.com

EXPERIENCE THE FASTEST GAME ON FOUR FEET

AT SARASOTA POLO CLUB

Did you know the oldest recorded team sport in known history is polo? Played on a 10-acre field of grass (about nine football fields, to give you perspective) polo is a fast-moving sport played on horseback. Similar in some ways to soccer, the object of the game is to move the ball down the field to make a goal. The difference is that a mallet is used to move the ball, and the player does this from a polo pony. The ponies are primarily thoroughbreds, considered to be the most athletic performers, so it's a fun game to watch. If you happen to be visiting during first quarter of the year, the Sarasota Polo Club hosts 15 weeks of polo matches, every Sunday at 1 p.m. In addition, from mid-March until around mid-April, Sunset Polo Happy Hour takes place every Thursday. Kids under 12 are free, so make it a family affair!

8201 Polo Club Ln., 941-907-0000
sarasotapolo.com

PLAY MINI GOLF AND FEED THE GATORS AT SMUGGLERS COVE

Yes, you can play mini golf just about anywhere, but at Smugglers Cove Adventure Golf, you can play golf with gators! At this 18-hole mini-style adventure golf course, home to 20 to 30 American alligators, you'll navigate your way through pirate ships, waterfalls, caves, and yes, real live alligators! What makes it different from mini golf? The challenges! Flowing water and surprises while you're playing are all part of the fun! There's a clubhouse and snack bar in case you get hungry or thirsty while playing—they even serve beer, wine, and hard seltzers. You won't find many places where you can play golf among gators and even get a chance to feed them, so be sure to stop by Smugglers Cove for a round or two, voted best mini golf in Florida five years in a row. Check the website for a discount code to save money on your next visit.

3815 N Tamiami Trl., 941-351-6620
smugglersgolf.com/sarasota

2000 Cortez Rd. W, Bradenton, 941-756-0043
smugglersgolf.com/bradenton

59

HELP SAVE
OUR SEABIRDS

At Save Our Seabirds, the organization's name says it all. If a wild bird is in trouble, it's Save Our Seabirds to the rescue, rehabilitation, and hopefully, release. For those birds that won't recover enough to be safely released, their forever home will be at Save Our Seabirds. Take a walk on the Birdwalk and meet the residents, learning about the different species, what makes them unique, as well as environmental risks and what we can do to minimize risks to our feathered friends. With 120-plus residents in the three-acre facility, you never know what kind of birds you might see. You will more than likely see Lady, the resident sandhill crane, who is a wonderful surrogate to orphaned babies, as well as cormorants, pelicans, vultures, seagulls, and owls. But depending on what is picked up from the 5,000 distress calls throughout the year, you could see hawks, roseate spoonbills, cardinals, and more.

1708 Ken Thompson Pkwy., 941-388-3010
saveourseabirds.org

TIP

Save Our Seabirds is just next door to Mote Marine Aquarium and there is no cost to visit, though donations are greatly appreciated.

SEE A LIVE WATER SKI SHOW

AT SKI-A-REES

There's a reason why Sarasota Ski-A-Rees has been a longstanding tradition since 1957. With a team of expert skiers performing stunts and tricks, this show is good old-fashioned family fun! In 1958, Cypress Gardens was contracted to organize and present a special ski show to be part of the Sarasota County Pageant. This event brought on the realization that there was a lot of interest in waterskiing. With the help of the City of Sarasota, private sponsors, and club members, the nonprofit Ski-A-Rees has been performing weekly water shows for almost 60 years. Take a seat on the bleachers or feel free to bring your own chairs. You'll find free parking as well as a concession stand for drinks and snacks. For those who would like to try waterskiing, Ski-A-Rees is a great place to learn. All skill levels are welcomed. Shows usually run from February through the first week of November on Sundays.

1602 Ken Thompson Pkwy., 941-388-1666
skiarees.com

TIP

The water ski shows are free, although donations are appreciated.

WATCH THE SUN SET
AT BEAN POINT

When I asked locals their favorite things to do, this was repeated over and over. Named after George Emerson Bean, the first settler of Anna Maria Island, Bean Point is a pristine and secluded portion of beautiful beach on the northern point of Anna Maria Island. Though George Emerson Bean passed away just six years after settling, his son had a hand in planning the design of the entire island. Bean Point is not only one of the top spots for watching that great orb sink into the body of water where the Gulf of Mexico meets Tampa Bay, but you'll also have a great view of the Sunshine SkyWay Bridge. In addition, this is a fantastic location for spotting dolphins, sea turtles, and other wildlife. Take your beach chairs, towels, and a snack, and enjoy a peaceful end to the day on Anna Maria Island.

793 N Shore Dr., Anna Maria
bradentongulfislands.com/discover/beaches

TIP

Watch for no-parking signs as you may get ticketed. The "main entrance" to Bean Point is a tree-lined path between two properties at the intersection of North Shore Drive and North Bay Boulevard. It is a bit of a walk along the sand and eventually a footbridge to get to the beach.

BE GUARANTEED TO SEE DOLPHINS IN THE WILD
WITH PARADISE BOAT TOURS

We have a lot of dolphins in the Sarasota-Bradenton area. Teams of researchers have been keeping track of the dolphins of Sarasota Bay since the early 1970s, and they know that around 150 identifiable dolphins make this area their home. They're protected by the Federal Marine Mammal Protection Act, and we can only hope their numbers continue to rise with awareness of the threats we pose to them, like boat traffic, fishing gear, and loss of habitat. To see these beautiful creatures in the wild, you need to know where they hang out. That's exactly what they do at Paradise Boat Tours. The gentle ride through the waters of Anna Maria was fun in itself, but we couldn't wait to see dolphins. Our guide said he had a good idea of where they would be, and he was right! Seeing so many playful dolphins frolicking in the waters of the bay was an unforgettable experience, and it's a must when visiting this area.

200 Bridge St., Bldg. A, Bradenton Beach, 941-465-8624
seedolphins.com

63

GET A BIRD'S-EYE VIEW OF THE CITY

WITH SARASOTA HELICOPTER TOURS

There's nothing like seeing a city from above, especially a city that's on the coast. Viewing that white sand and turquoise water from the comfort of your seat in a helicopter? That's the trip of a lifetime and one you'll want to take while visiting Sarasota. Whether you're looking for a thrill ride, a sightseeing exploration, or a romantic place to propose, a doors-off helicopter ride with Sarasota Helicopter Tours will be a ride to remember. You'll meet Mark, your pilot and the owner of the company, at Sarasota Airport. Your ride will be either an orange or blue Robinson R44 Raven II. Spend a little time on your safety briefing, and get ready to climb up over the city. On Sarasota Helicopter Tours, you can see the entire coastline from Anna Maria Island to Venice, or design a custom tour of your own for up to three people.

1234 Clyde Jones Rd., 941-800-1515
sarasotahelicoptertour.com

SOAK IN TWO-MILLION-YEAR-OLD WATER
AT WARM MINERAL SPRINGS

Though it's about a 40-minute drive to visit Warm Mineral Springs Park in North Port, how often in your life are you able to soak in two-million-year-old water? Warm Mineral Springs Park is an 81.6-acre warm springs park with an average year-round temperature of 85 degrees Fahrenheit, and the only publicly accessible warm springs in all of Florida. Here's your chance to wade where saber-toothed tigers and giant sloths walked. Besides being a cool thing to do, soaking in the springs is also therapeutic. As the springs arguably contain the highest mineral content of any natural spring in all of the country, it's believed soaking in the minerals has healing properties. The Warm Mineral Springs Park is listed in the US National Register of Historic Places, giving you yet another reason to visit. Why not take a picnic and make a whole day of it?

12200 San Servando Ave., North Port, 941-429-7275
northportfl.gov/community-recreation/parks-facilities/warm-mineral-springs-park

65

SEE MANATEES IN THE WILD

AT THE MANATEE VIEWING CENTER AT APOLLO BEACH

I remember visiting the Sarasota-Bradenton area before moving here and asking over and over, where can I see manatees? If only I had known about the Manatee Viewing Center! Every time I've visited this 63-acre nature preserve in Hillsborough County, I've seen several manatees as well as stingrays. Once we saw a shark jump right out of the water! In addition to wildlife viewing, seven acres of the preserve are for recreation, so bring a picnic and enjoy sunbathing, bird-watching, a short nature trail, an observation tower, and great shoreline fishing. Named one of the *USA Today* 10Best Readers' Choice best free attractions, this is one you really should not miss. Of course, there's always a chance you'll see a manatee in the bay or gulf waters during the summer, but during winter, follow the manatees to the warm waters of Tampa Electric's state and federally designated sanctuary.

6990 Dickman Rd., Apollo Beach, 813-228-4289
tampaelectric.com/manatee

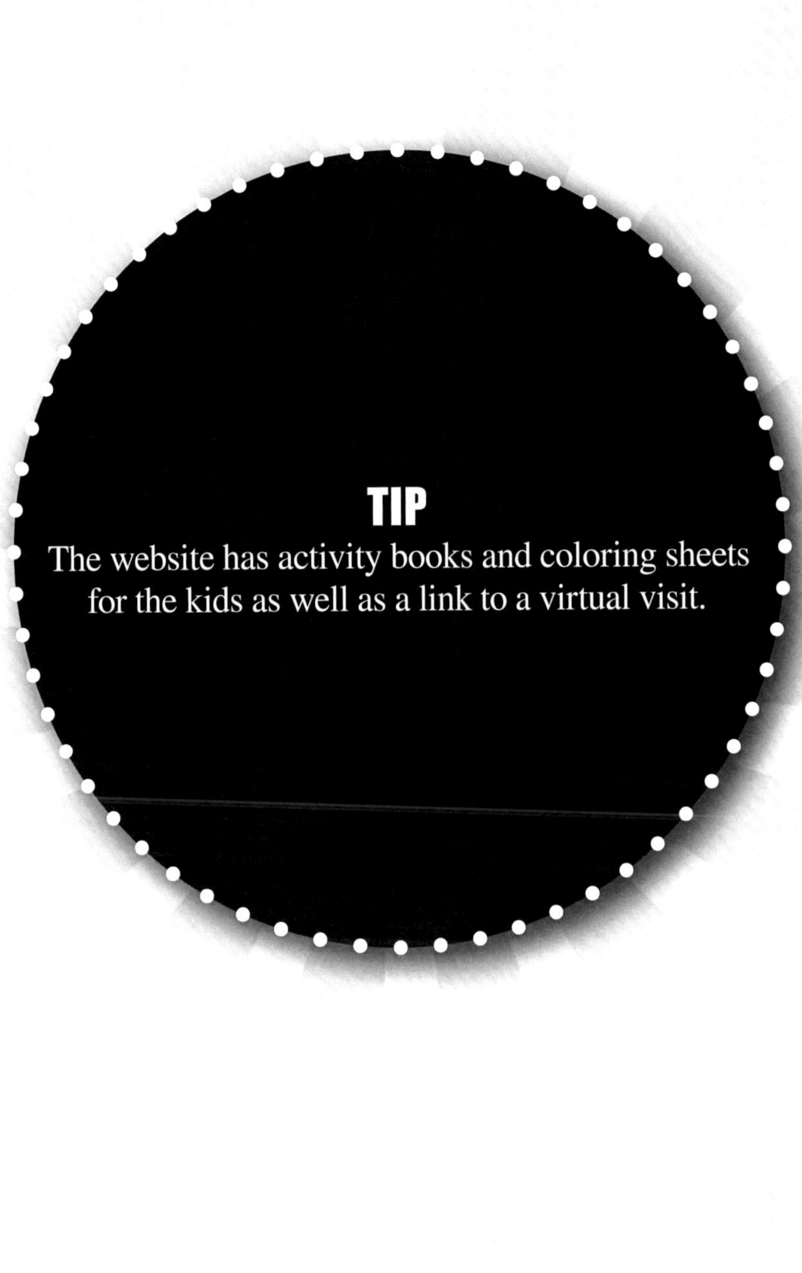
TIP
The website has activity books and coloring sheets for the kids as well as a link to a virtual visit.

FLOAT IN AN LED GLASS-BOTTOM BOAT AT NIGHT

WITH FUN FLORIDA TOURS

Ever wonder what wildlife you might see in the gulf at night? Here's your chance to find out! Fun Florida Tours has clear glass-bottom tandem kayaks with 10,000 lumens of LED glow and will take you on a tour under the stars. Though there is no guarantee you'll see wildlife, you know it's out there, so there's always a good chance. On past tours guests have seen manatees, fish, dolphins, stingrays, conch, and other marine life. Nervous? Don't be! The knowledgeable tour guides will help you get comfortable in the kayak or with the paddleboard. Why not get outside and do something different with your family and friends? This would make a great date night, too. Day tours, paddleboard tours, and even sunset tours are available. Each tour has its own charm, like the mangrove tunnels on Anna Maria Island. Tours in our area include Sarasota, Siesta Key, and Anna Maria Island.

941-259-9713
funfltours.com

67

GET TOASTED (COCONUT)
AT SIESTA KEY RUM DISTILLERY

First things first. Siesta Key Rum distillery is not in Siesta Key, so don't start out on your journey heading that way. The distillery is actually in Sarasota. We won't hold that against them, because their rums are worth traveling for. We recommend a tasting, one of which will be toasted coconut. This would be perfect in a rum cake, and we can't wait to try it out! The Siesta Key Rum distillery uses no artificial flavorings to make those flavorful spirits, which are perfect for sipping or creating something scrumptious. The tasting is free and makes for a fun stop. After you explore all their varieties, head back to the bar that was once located in Bahi Hut (see #27). Check out the sign on the wall with the bar's history. Why not make your next stop the Bahi Hut? It's only a seven-minute drive and worth seeing!

2212 Industrial Blvd., 941-702-8143
siestakeyrum.com

TIP

Check Florida Craft Spirits for our local Distillery Trail.
floridacraftspirits.org/florida-distillery-trail

GRAB YOUR SNORKEL
AND SEE WHAT YOU CAN FIND

There's a lot to see in the beautiful, clear waters of our area, so grab your snorkel and explore! Popular snorkeling spots include Turtle and Crescent Beaches in Sarasota as well as Holmes and Bradenton Beaches in Bradenton. Don't have a snorkel? Just about every shop near the beach has them. Pick up sunscreen, too. If you've never tried a snorkel, familiarize yourself with it before going into the water. Many people snorkel right from the shore. Things you might see include tropical fish, starfish, crab, and sea stars. Though our waters are calm, parents must keep an eye on their children as it's easy to drift out with the waves. In addition, dolphins have been known to come in close to the shore, especially near a pier. And never ever take anything out of the water. Starfish and sand dollars are living creatures and will die once out of the water.

TIP

During the warmer months of May through October, you could encounter stingrays in shallow water. Stepping on a stingray can be painful, so instead of lifting your feet as you walk through the water, do the "Stingray Shuffle" and slide your feet without lifting them.

SAIL AWAY
ON THE MARINA JACK SUNSET DINNER CRUISE

If a sunset dinner cruise is on your bucket list, Sarasota is the place to do it! This cruise is a relaxing way to spend an evening. The narrated cruise takes you through the waters of the Intracoastal Waterway and the Gulf of Mexico. You'll board the 96-foot cruise vessel behind Marina Jack restaurant on the bayfront in downtown Sarasota. You'll often see dolphins and other wildlife while you sail along. There is comfortable inside seating with air-conditioning as well as outdoor seating for alfresco dining. The dinner cruise includes a buffet of carved prime rib, salmon, as well as several sides and dessert. A full bar is available as well, and lunch cruises and sightseeing cruises are also offered. Kids are welcome for this family-friendly cruise. A dinner cruise is a great way to celebrate an anniversary or birthday. Reserve your dates early to guarantee seating!

2 Marina Plz., 941-955-9488
marinajacks.com/sightseeing-cruises

70

CYCLE

THE LEGACY TRAIL

The riding is easy on Sarasota's Legacy Trail, the 18.2-mile car-free paved public park that runs between Venice Train Depot and Payne Park in Sarasota. Join your neighbors exercising, skating, hiking, or just walking their dog. Rail trails are becoming more and more popular across the country, with 25,000 miles converted so far. The Legacy Trail is part of the Rails to Trails Conservancy, turning former railroad corridors into public paths for recreation. Both Venice Train Depot and Payne Park have a circus-themed playground, a nod to the family who put Sarasota on the map. Legacy Park, across from the Venice Train Depot, also has a canoe and kayak launch, drinking fountains, and picnic shelters. Payne Park has picnic tables and a water fountain, as well as food and beverages at Cafe in the Park. See the website for other places you can join the trail.

sarasotacountyparks.com/parks-and-facilities/discover-a-park/destination-parks/the-legacy-trail

> **TIP**
>
> You can track your progress and save your favorites on TrailLink, the Rails to Trails Conservancy's desktop or mobile app.

71

GO GLAMPING
AT OSCAR SCHERER STATE PARK

If glamping has been on your bucket list, here's your chance to check it off! Glamping is camping made luxurious, with upscale amenities like proper linens, a phone charger, a Keurig coffee maker, a mini fridge, and heating or air-conditioning. A nearby shared bathhouse has restrooms and showers. Have that first cup of coffee on the front porch, just steps from your comfy bed, and listen to the sounds of nature. Get out and explore 15 miles of trails. After a hike, come back and relax before you head out for more adventurous fun like kayaking or cycling the Legacy Trail. As for wildlife, bald eagles nest there in winter. In summer, you'll probably see Florida scrub jays among the 200 local bird species. You may also see otters and alligators. At the end of the day, fire up the charcoal grill, make dinner, and enjoy it alfresco under the string lights followed by roasting marshmallows over the wood firepit.

1843 S Tamiami Trl., 941-777-3114
sarasota.tlglamping.com

Manatee Village Historical Park

CULTURE AND HISTORY

SEE THE GREATEST SHOW ON EARTH IN MINIATURE

AT THE RINGLING

If you've ever been to the circus, you probably remember trying to watch what was happening in all three rings at once. Imagine seeing the entire circus—including behind the scenes where performers ate, slept, and practiced—all laid out for you to explore. With 44,000 pieces, you've never seen the circus like this. The Howard Bros. Circus Model is the world's largest miniature circus, covering 3,800 square feet. This replica of Ringling Bros. and Barnum & Bailey Circus will thrill young and old alike. And if that isn't enough excitement to bring you to the Ringling, you can also see Ca' d'Zan, the 36,000-square-foot mansion the Ringlings built; the spectacular Ringling Museum of Art; and the Bayfront Gardens with Mable Ringling's lovely Rose Garden. Plan to spend the day. The Ringling Grillroom is a fabulous on-site restaurant with an upscale menu as well as beer, wine, and cocktails.

5401 Bayshore Rd., 941-359-5700
ringling.org

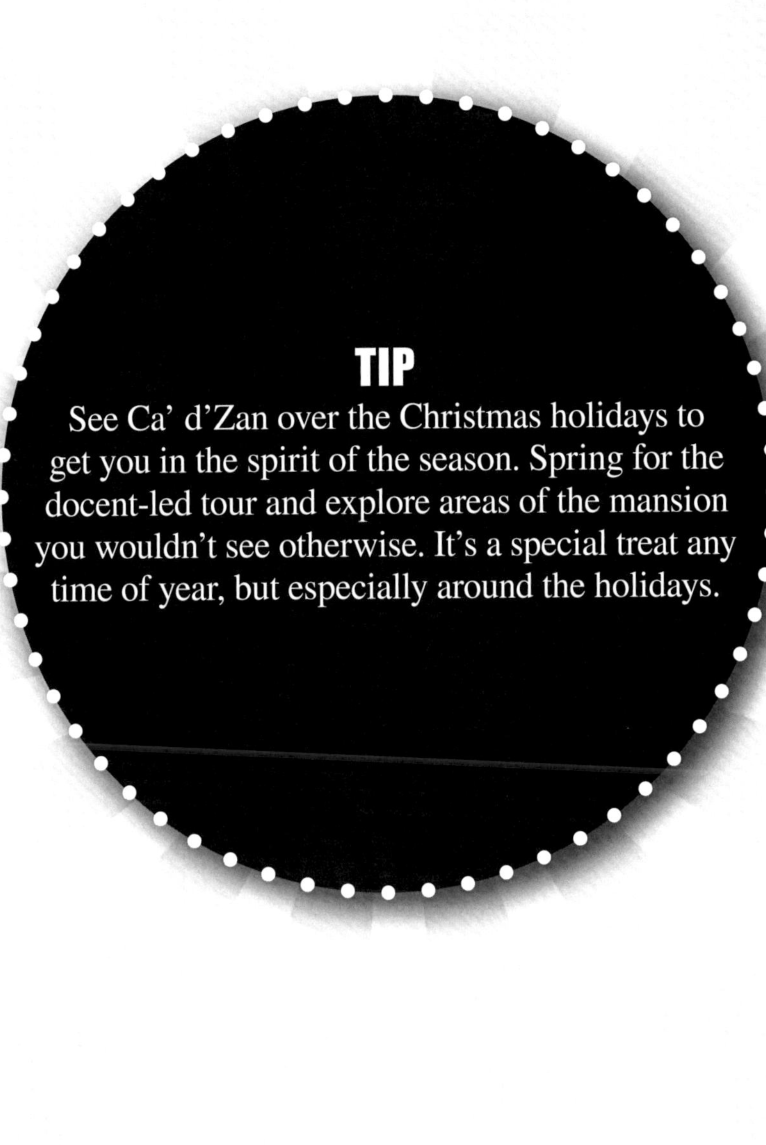

TIP

See Ca' d'Zan over the Christmas holidays to get you in the spirit of the season. Spring for the docent-led tour and explore areas of the mansion you wouldn't see otherwise. It's a special treat any time of year, but especially around the holidays.

73

STOP AND SMELL THE ORCHIDS

AT MARIE SELBY BOTANICAL GARDENS

One of Sarasota's treasures, Marie Selby Gardens is as picturesque as you'd imagine. With two locations within 10 miles of one another, you can easily see both in a day. The downtown Sarasota location offers 15 acres of exploration along Sarasota Bay. Take a walk along the bayfront mangrove walkway. Walk through a tropical rainforest or desert. Explore the native Florida area, or stand in awe before the majestic Banyon Grove. Children will love playing in the Children's Rainforest Garden with swinging bridges and a 12-foot waterfall. Fans of Florida history will enjoy the Spanish Point location, where you can visit the White Cottage built in 1884 and see the sunken gardens and pergola with a fabulous view of Sarasota Bay. View early pioneer life at Guptill House, and take a walk through the Victorian-style garden at Duchene Lawn. Children can learn about citrus packing and even give it a try at Webb Packing House.

1534 Mound St., 941-366-5731
401 N Tamiami Trl., Osprey, 941-366-5731
selby.org/visit

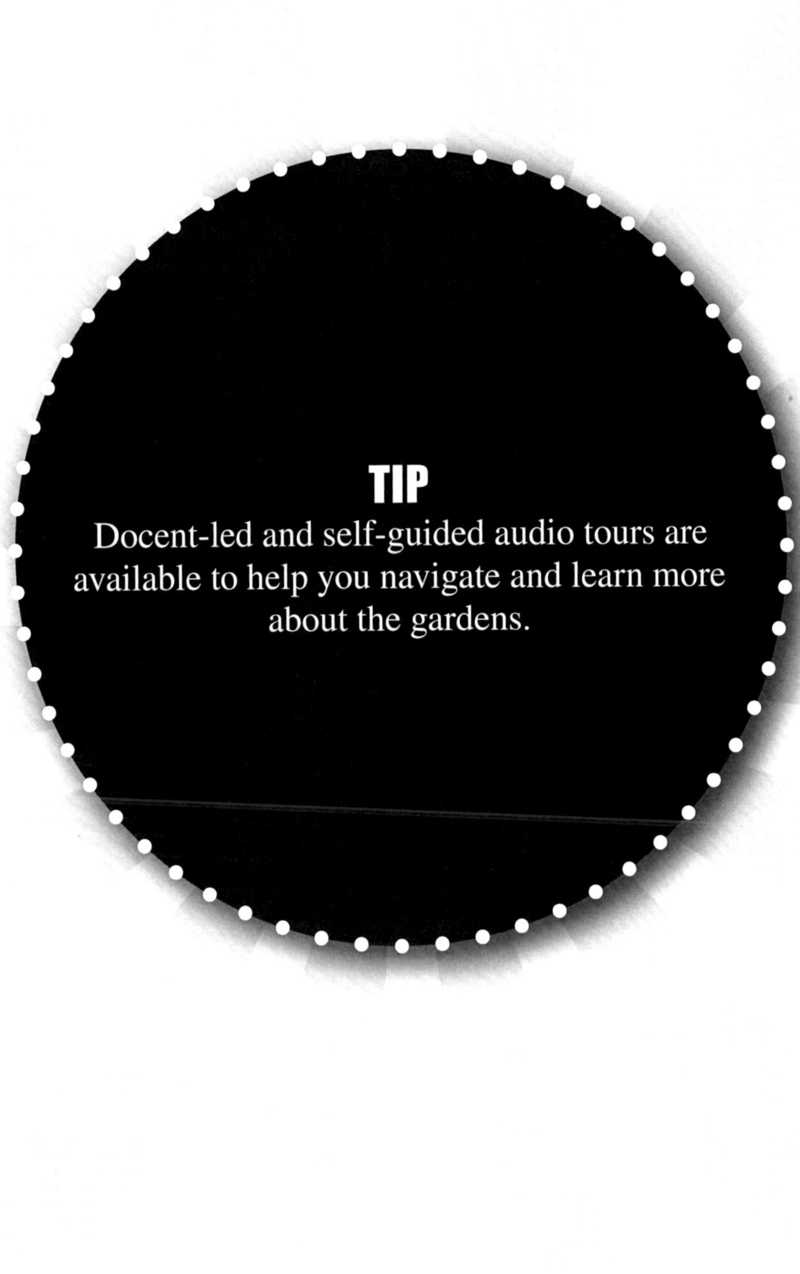
TIP
Docent-led and self-guided audio tours are available to help you navigate and learn more about the gardens.

74

SAVOR YOUR WAY AROUND THE AREA

WITH A TOUR FROM KEY CULINARY TOURS

With so many fantastic restaurants in our area, where do you begin? One way to start is by booking a food tour with Key Culinary Tours. I've done many food tours all over the world, and it's a great way to get a taste of some of the top restaurants as well as to learn a little history from a local tour guide. With tours in Sarasota, St. Armands Circle, Anna Maria Island, and Venice, it's easy to find something close to you. Many tours are available, focusing on breakfast or brunch, lunch, dinner, and even wine tours! If you prefer a tour for just the history, Key Culinary Tours also has a Shark's Teeth Tour, Wild Women of Sarasota Tours, and even Ghost Tours! Guides are local residents who know the area. Have an idea for a tour? Contact them to set up a custom tour just for your group.

1727 Fruitville Rd., 941-893-4664
keyculinarytours.com

GO BACK IN TIME
AT MANATEE VILLAGE HISTORICAL PARK

In 1974, a group of women were told their church, built in 1887, as well as a smaller building that was once Manatee County's first courthouse, would be torn down. They made a decision to save the two historic buildings and took the steps to organize the then-defunct Manatee County Historical Commission with a goal of preserving Manatee County's pioneer history.

This four-acre historical park was created to showcase Manatee County's heritage from 1840 through 1918. You'll find a lot to explore, including the 1913 Old Cabbage Head locomotive, Wiggins Store, Stephens House, and nearby, the 1850 Manatee Burying Ground. Tours are self-led, but the museum does have activities such as a picture-based scavenger hunt, activity books for children 8 and up, a history and artifacts challenge, and monthly lectures for adults. For more information, ask in the Wiggins Store. After touring the park, kids can get the wiggles out on the playground.

1404 Manatee Ave. E, Bradenton, 941-749-7165
manateevillage.org

TIP

Two apps are available on the website to help with your self-led tour.

REVISIT THE ROARING '20S THROUGH THE HIDDEN SPEAKEASY DOOR

AT DIVE WINE & SPIRITS

You have to wonder if someone has given you the wrong address for a speakeasy when you walk into Dive Wine & Spirits. Of course, that's the idea. Walk through the aisles to the back of the store and you'll see a freezer door. Don't be shy. Go ahead and open it. Welcome to Dive Cocktail Den, a fun, Florida-style speakeasy. The lights are low, and the bar's shelves are backlit with black lights. Join new friends at the bar. There are couches and chairs and fun decor based on diving and the sea. Pick up the tropical-themed menu and choose something delicious like the Passionfruit Mule or a Jungle Bird. Dive Wine & Spirits also hosts special events at their Hive Bar, just to the right of the store entrance. You never know what to expect, and I get the feeling that's just the way they want it.

2881 Clark Rd., 941-888-0382
diveliquors.com

TIP
Check out their Tacos & Tequila Night,
Pasta & Wine Night, and Pop-Up Food Pairings.

77

EXPLORE SCIENCE AND NATURE
AT THE BISHOP MUSEUM

The whole family will enjoy a visit to the largest natural and cultural museum on the Gulf Coast of Florida. See fossils of Florida's earliest animals and learn about the archaeological history of the state in the first-floor permanent exhibits. Kids will love the Mosaic Backyard Universe, fully accessible and created for kids of all ages. The second floor offers an opportunity to see something new each time you visit as the collection is rotated. The River Heritage Hall exhibits the cultural history of the Manatee River and Tampa Bay. Don't miss the Parker Manatee Rehabilitation Habitat with over and underwater viewing of these gentle creatures, all rescues. Environmental Hall sheds light on environmental awareness for our region. The Full Dome Planetarium, the Gulf Coast's premier astronomy facility, is where to go to learn about the stars in a dark-sky environment. Learn about black holes, comets, and asteroids. Entrance to the planetarium is included with admission.

201 10th St. W, Bradenton, 941-746-4131
bishopscience.org

TIP

Be sure to check the calendar for events like Laser Light Nights as well as special exhibits.

WATCH
HERRMANN'S ROYAL LIPIZZAN HORSES TRAIN

Unless you're planning to visit the Spanish Riding School in Vienna, Austria, to see the Lipizzaners perform, don't miss your chance to see Herrmann's Royal Lipizzans in action. Located in Myakka City, about 40 minutes outside of the Sarasota-Bradenton area, you can watch these remarkable horses and riders practice every Thursday, Friday, and Saturday as they prance around the fenced arena. Sitting on the benches in the morning sunshine, it's hard to believe you're watching a tradition that goes back to the 16th century. The Herrmann family came to the United States in 1962 with three Lipizzan horses, one of the rarest breeds in the world with an estimated 8,000 remaining. The Herrmanns are dedicated to promoting and preserving the breed and are now in their fifth generation of riders. After the show, guests are invited to the stalls to see the stallions and mares up close. It really is a bucket-list experience, right in our own backyard.

32755 Singletary Rd., Myakka City, 941-322-1501
herrmannsroyallipizzans.com

TIP

Reservations are strongly suggested for groups of 20 or more.

79

TAKE
A SARASOTA TROLLEY TOUR

Learn about the history and culture of Sarasota from an experienced tour guide while being driven around town in the comfortable and air-conditioned "Dolly the Trolley." On the City Sightseeing Tour, you'll hear stories about the Ringling family and the history of the circus, learn about Sarasota's Amish culture, and get ideas for shopping and dining after the tour. This 90-minute experience gives you a great overview of the city. I learned so much on my tour and can't wait to experience another one! Many other tours are available, including a Public Art Tour, an Architechtural Tour, an Amish Experience Tour, and even a Murder Mystery Trolley! Advance reservations are highly encouraged as tours often fill up early. All available tours are listed on their website. Unfortunately, strollers or wheelchairs cannot be accommodated on the trolley. No children under 10 are allowed on tours unless it's a specific holiday family-friendly tour.

1826 4th St., 941-260-9818
discoversarasotatours.com

VISIT SARASOTA'S PIECE OF THE FLORIDA HISTORIC GOLF TRAIL

Golf enthusiasts can't miss the Bobby Jones Golf Club. Sarasota has long been considered "the cradle of American golf." For starters, after moving to Sarasota from Scotland in 1886, John Hamilton Gillespie, future first mayor of Sarasota, decided to lay out a practice course of two greens and a fairway located between what is now Ringling Boulevard and Main Street. This two-hole course was the first golf course in Florida and the second in the United States. Over the years, more holes, a practice range, and a clubhouse were added. The course was sold and developed in 1923, and no sign of it remains. However, the land that Gillespie cleared when first taking over Florida Mortgage and Investment Company is where the Bobby Jones Golf Club sits today. Designed by Donald Ross in 1925, it is where Bobby Jones won the Grand Slam, all four majors in one year, a feat that hasn't been repeated yet by any golfer.

1000 Circus Blvd., 941-365-4653
bobbyjonesgolfclub.com

81

WALK THROUGH AN 1880S FISHING VILLAGE
IN CORTEZ

The Village of Cortez is a historic fishing village still active today. According to the not-for-profit Cortez Village Historical Society, which helped recognize Cortez as a historical landmark, it's one of the last active fishing villages remaining on the Gulf Coast of Florida. It was settled in the 1880s, and many of the descendants of the original settlers still live there today. Visitors can learn about the history of the village, including the effect of wars, hurricanes, and the Great Depression. See why elephants from Ringling Circus paraded across the Cortez Bridge when it first opened. Ninety-seven of the buildings in Cortez, such as the 1912 Rural Graded Schoolhouse, now housing the Florida Maritime Museum, are on the National Register of Historic Places. In 2016, the Cortez Cultural Center opened to display photos, furniture, clothing, and even sound bites documenting life in Cortez from the 1886 settlement. Be sure to stop for lunch or dinner at Star Fish Company or Tide Tables!

11655 Cortez Rd. W, Cortez, 941-840-0590
cortezvillagehistoricalsociety.org

WANDER THROUGH THE REGION'S FIRST CONTEMPORARY ART MUSEUM

AT SARASOTA ART MUSEUM

When it comes to the arts, Sarasota has a lot to offer, but it wasn't until 2019 that the city could boast a museum of contemporary art. It was a long time in the making, as the group of 13 Sarasotans who hoped to see the Sarasota Art Museum come to pass first met in 2003. All good things take time, and today visitors can explore 20th- and 21st-century art through exhibitions, an outdoor sculpture garden, and more. The museum is located in the 1926 late Gothic–style building that served as Sarasota High School until 1996 when classes began moving to other schools; we can't think of a better venue. Though the museum has 15,000 dedicated square feet of space for exhibitions, none of them are permanent, so there is always something new to see. Check the website for current exhibitions, special events, family activities, and free admission days.

1001 S Tamiami Trl., 941-309-4300
sarasotaartmuseum.org

83

TAKE A SELFIE
WITH THE *UNCONDITIONAL SURRENDER* STATUE

Sarasotans are very passionate about this statue, but it's received its share of controversy, too. Though the 25-foot, computer-generated, Styrofoam statue was first installed temporarily in Sarasota in 2005, it was moved to San Diego's Tuna Harbor Park two years later, also temporarily. Critics called it kitsch, but the public liked it. In fact, the USS *Midway* Museum led a fundraising campaign and came up with $1 million in eight weeks to have a bronze statue made, where it still stands. In 2009, Sarasota decided they wanted a copy of the statue back at the bayfront, so an aluminum copy was installed, again, temporarily. In 2012, a car struck the statue, putting a three-foot hole in the bottom. It was re-erected in the same spot later that year. In 2021, *Unconditional Surrender* was moved to its current home in between O'Leary's Tiki Bar and Marina Jack, where you can take that selfie.

Bayfront Park, 5 Bayfront Dr., 941-263-6386
letsplaysarasota.com/parks

STROLL THROUGH
THE QUIRKY MARIETTA MUSEUM OF ART & WHIMSY

After visiting the Marietta Museum of Art & Whimsy, you'll wonder why every city doesn't have such a happy place. Founder and owner of the museum Marietta Lee was an emergency room nurse, seeing things that are unimaginable to most people. After one call to assist in an airplane crash where all five passengers had died, she knew she needed to make a change. She moved to Florida in 1984, and in 1991 earned a Bachelor of Fine Arts from Ringling College of Art and Design. Realizing that the amount of humorous art and art created by women were both lacking, she decided to do something about it. She also learned that, in life, sometimes we just need a break from worries and responsibilities. In 2010, the Marietta Museum of Art & Whimsy opened, filled with sculptures, paintings, and mixed media. Stop by and explore. You'll be sure to leave with a smile on your face.

2121 N Tamiami Trl., 941-364-3399
whimsymuseum.org

85

EXPERIENCE AN OLD-FASHIONED TRAIN RIDE
AT FLORIDA RAILROAD MUSEUM

Train buffs as well as parents of young kids will not want to miss a trip to the Florida Railroad Museum. With a variety of train rides, this is the way to see how the railroad existed back in the 1940s and '50s. It's also your chance to ride on the first train line through Manatee County. The train chugs along from Parrish to Willow along a now abandoned six-mile track. The trains are diesel powered and consist of open-air, open-window, and air-conditioned cars. Choose from different varieties of rides from the Willow Express to the Train Robbery Experience, where your train gets robbed by the Hole-in-the-Head Gang. Kids will love the Cotton Tail Special Easter Egg Hunt, and families will enjoy the Hobo Campfire Cookout, which includes hot dogs and marshmallows. You can even rent the Party Caboose, a fun party venue for a birthday or other event.

12210 83rd St. E, Parrish, 941-776-0906
frrm.org

BE ENTERTAINED BY REGIONAL TALENT
AT FLORIDA STUDIO THEATRE

In 2023, Florida Studio Theatre (FST) celebrated 50 years of bringing quality regional entertainment to Sarasota. FST is currently the largest subscription theatre in the state and among the largest in the US, and with so much diversity in performances there's something for everyone. The Winter Main Stage offers Tony Award–winning plays like *The Lehman Trilogy* and the cult classic *Little Shop of Horrors*. At the Winter Caberet you'll see shows with music, song, and dance, like the *Up On the Roof Revival* featuring tunes from the 1950s and 1960s and the guitar musical revue *Take It To The Limit*, a tribute to 1970s rock and roll. For those who prefer more innovative entertainment, check out the plays in Stage III or the shows in FST Improv. Florida Studio Theatre even has a Children's Theatre Series featuring shows like *Red Riding Hood*, *The Velveteen Rabbit*, and *Deck the Halls*, perfect for getting families into the holiday spirit.

TIP

With subscription savings of up to 50 percent, becoming a subscriber can save you a bundle over regular single-ticket prices.

The Bazaar on Apricot & Lime,
photo courtesy of Kim Livengood

SHOPPING AND FASHION

87

GET READY FOR WATER SPORTS
WITH CB'S SALTWATER OUTFITTERS

If you're planning time on the water, you'll need equipment, and CB's Saltwater Outfitters has just about everything when it comes to water-related activities. Though known as the largest bait and tackle shop in Siesta Key, they have so much more than fishing rods, hooks, and worms! Looking to rent a Jet Ski, boat, or go parasailing? Want to take your whole gang on a chartered boat ride? Give them a call and set it up. If a tiki boat tour is more your style, they're offered every day. Didn't really dress for fishing or a boat ride? They've got popular name-brand sportswear for men and women. You can even rent a golf cart for a half day, full day, or by the week. When visiting this area of the Gulf Coast, CB's Saltwater Outfitters really has you covered for all your saltwater needs. There's a reason they've been in business since 1959.

1249 Stickney Point Rd., Siesta Key, 941-349-4400
cbsoutfitters.com

VISIT AN INDIE INDOOR MARKET

AT THE BAZAAR ON APRICOT & LIME

Shop from 40 local curators in one building at the Bazaar on Apricot & Lime. From handmade furniture and clothing to handcrafted jewelry, collectibles, and even one-of-a-kind items, this is your one-stop gift shop in Sarasota. The Bazaar thinks shopping should be fun, which is why you'll enjoy live music most days from noon until 3 p.m. Sign up for an art class. Kiss the puppies at their adoption events. Shop for the holidays during their Christmas in July. And don't miss their 3rd Saturday Limelight Pop-Up Market. Be sure to check out their Facebook page to see what's going on when you're planning to visit. And don't worry about stopping to eat beforehand. Hamlet's Eatery is their on-site award-winning food truck serving up everything from breakfast burritos to tacos to burgers. Craft beer and wine are also on the menu. Enjoy it all in the outdoor garden. Sounds like the perfect girls' day out to me!

821 Apricot Ave., 941-445-1938
bazaaronapricotandlime.com

EXPERIENCE A BIT OF VENICE, ITALY, IN VENICE, FLORIDA,
AT COPPOLA ARTISTICA

Venice, Florida, was originally designed in the Italian Renaissance style back in the 1920s after a citrus farmer said it reminded him of the city's European namesake. Walking into Coppola Artistica is truly like walking into a ceramics shop in Venice, Italy. The pieces are exquisite, imported not just from Venice but from many different regions of Italy. In fact, the owner's grandparents were in the ceramics business in Italy, and his mother, who had two stores of her own in Italy, helped select most of the items in the store. You'll find everything from wall art to vases to garlic graters. And though the items are pricey, they are imported, so think of it as saving the airfare. I found a beautiful olive oil cruet and spoon rest I'm still thinking about, so I will probably be paying them another visit soon. The pitchers are gorgeous, too. Make sure to stop in and tell them we sent you.

213 W Venice Ave., Ste. B, Venice, 941-484-8739
ebay.com/str/coppolaartimports2014

SHOP UNTIL YOU DROP
AT GINNY & JANE E'S

Is it a store or a restaurant? When these two sisters decided to open a store together, they knew they needed something big enough for Ginny's love of retail decor and Jane's passion for baking. They found the old IGA store that had been run by Ernie Cagnina, a former mayor of Anna Maria, and fortunately his family was willing to see the store given new life. Located right on Gulf Drive on Anna Maria Island, this is where to take visitors to pick up gifts for friends and family. Filled with all kinds of tropical decor, funky art, handmade jewelry, postcards, and souvenirs, Ginny & Jane E's is an institution. And if you're hungry, head to the back for one of their famous cinnamon rolls. They're large enough to share and so delicious. Ginny & Jane E's is open for breakfast and lunch. Is it a store or a restaurant? It's definitely both!

9807 Gulf Dr., Anna Maria, 941-778-3170
ginnysandjanees.com

91

FIND THE PERFECT GIFT AND MORE

AT CROWDER'S GIFTS & GADGETS

This upscale gift shop has everything from Brighton handbags and jewelry to candles and greeting cards. My eyes glaze over with all the things I want in their section for housewares. Lovely platters, place mats, and pretty napkins that change out with the seasons adorn the shelves. You'll also find wineglasses and accessories. In the back, you'll find rows of greeting cards, including the ones that make you laugh until you cry. Find candles of many colors, designs, and scents. Explore the section of personal-care items like lotions, body wash, and hand creams. To the right of the entrance there's a section of clothing including shoes. Finally, Crowder's is known for Grandma Crowder's Homemade Fudge, including seasonal varieties that often sell out. This is the perfect shop for gifts. It really is an eclectic mix of items, and I always leave with something!

5409 Manatee Ave. W, Bradenton, 941-795-2442
2401 Lakewood Ranch Blvd., Lakewood Ranch, 941-744-2442
crowdersgifts.com

GET LOST
AT THE RED BARN FLEA MARKET

If you really like to shop local, this is a fun place to do it! If you've ever driven along First Street east in Bradenton, you've undoubtedly seen the very big red barn. With 600 flea market booths over 20 acres, you can easily spend the day here. You'll find a traditional flea market experience along with regular shops, as well as open-air farmers markets with some of the freshest fruits and veggies around, all at great prices! In addition, uncover that something you've been searching for at the Garage Sale booths, discover 10 art murals adorning the walls, and grab a bite at one of the food courts. Worried about the heat or rain? Leave your worries behind because Red Barn has 80,000 square feet of indoor shopping! Check out the live music every Friday and Saturday. Plan to spend the day. Check the website for special and holiday events.

1707 1st St. E, Bradenton, 941-747-3794 or 1-800-274-3532
redbarnfleamarket.com

TIP

The Mexican food stalls are incredible for authentic Mexican dishes, so be sure to stay for lunch or dinner.

93

FIND A SPECIAL SOUVENIR

AT SEA PLEASURES AND TREASURES

Have you ever walked into a store and instantly known it was special? You wouldn't be the first if you felt that way after walking into Sea Pleasures and Treasures. As a matter of fact, visitors to this shop often tell the friendly staff stories of when they visited with their parents as they watch their children look wide-eyed at the fossils and gemstones. That happens when you've been in business for 60 years. There's so much to see at this shop, you'll want to take your time. Much of it is Florida-themed, such as shark teeth, seashells, beach accessories, jewelry, and T-shirts. You'll also find beach-themed tableware and glasses, perfect for dining on your lanai. Don't miss the display of megalodon shark teeth and Ice Age mammals found right in Venice. The Green Parrot Gift Shop, just a couple of stores away, is their fun sister store.

255 W Venice Ave., Venice, 941-488-3510
visitvenicefl.org/places/sea-pleasures-treasures

PICK UP GOURMET OLIVE OIL (AND MORE)

AT THE ANCIENT OLIVE GOURMET

This is personally one of my favorite stores, and it's a must when I'm visiting St. Armands Circle.

The main draw here is olive oil, and with more than 25 varieties to choose from, it's easy to see why. I can think of a multitude of recipes to use chipotle, garlic, and herbs de Provence–infused olive oils. All the oils have suggestions for how to use them, and you'll find recipes on the store's website. Ancient Olive Gourmet also has a plethora of balsamic vinegars, from Black Mission Fig to Chocolate di Torino. But man does not live on oil and vinegar alone, so you'll also find gourmet crackers, seasonings, jams, several varieties of pesto, pastas, cocktail mixers, and even gourmet coffee. And because you'll need pretty dishes to serve all the amazing foods you'll be making with your purchases, they have those, too. See? This store is just a party in the making!

26 N Blvd. of the Presidents, 941-388-1414
theancientolive.com

95

TASTE YOUR WAY TO YOUR NEW FAVORITE CHEESE

AT ARTISAN CHEESE COMPANY

I can't think of a better way to buy cheese than to be able to read the descriptions and ask for a taste. From Fort Saint Antione Comté to Prairie Breeze Cheddar, where the milk is produced on small family farms, there is so much to choose from at the Artisan Cheese Company. That's why tasting the cheese, with the description right next to your tiny cutting board of tastings, is so helpful. I had no idea I would like the smoky flavor of Piper's Pyramid until it was served on a cheese board. Yes, you can order a cheese board and the staff will choose a few cheeses and pair them perfectly with accoutrements like fig spread, fruit, and crackers. And yes, you can pair with a glass of wine, as well. What a wonderful way to shop! Artisan Cheese Company is open for lunch and is happy to cater your next gathering.

550 Central Ave., 941-951-7860
artisancheesecompany.com

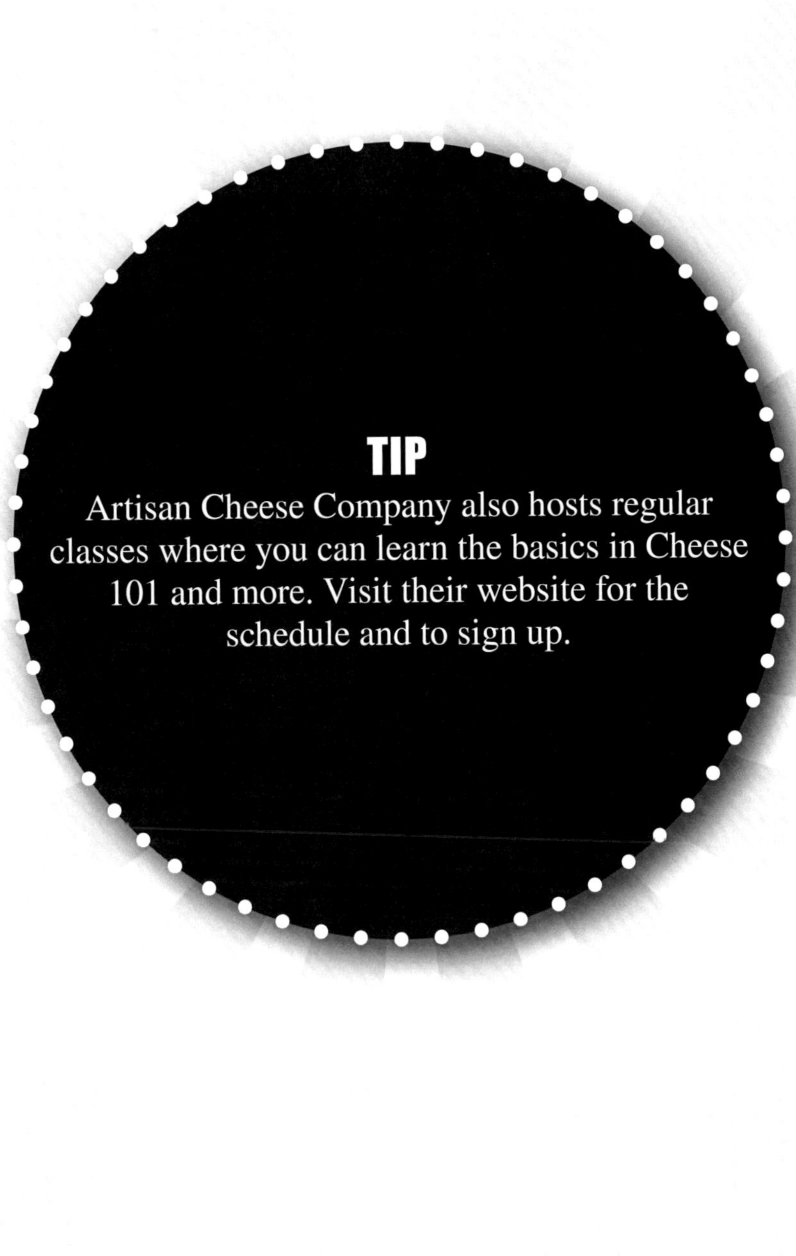
TIP
Artisan Cheese Company also hosts regular classes where you can learn the basics in Cheese 101 and more. Visit their website for the schedule and to sign up.

SHOP TO YOUR HEART'S CONTENT INDOORS
AT UNIVERSITY TOWN CENTER

When you feel like shopping indoors or know exactly what you need, the Mall at University Town Center is the place to go. With more than 100 stores, you're sure to find just what you're looking for and more. Department stores Macy's and Dillard's flank either ends of the mall with smaller stores lining the first and second levels. From fashion to decor and home goods to shoes and makeup, you'll really find it all at UTC. An Apple Store can be found mid-mall. For birthday parties or special occasions, a Build-A-Bear Workshop is located near the children's play area by Dillard's. And speaking of kids, you'll find stores with clothing just for little ones, like Cotton On Kids and Carter's. Stop and get a bite to eat at one of the 20-plus dining options.

140 University Town Center Dr., 941-552-7000
mallatutc.com

TIP

If you're an Apple iPhone user, download the Mall at UTC app for directions as well as sales and special events.

STOCK UP ON LOCAL PRODUCE AND MORE

AT THE FARMERS MARKET AT LAKEWOOD RANCH

A visit to the Farmers Market at Lakewood Ranch is a must. It's where you can pick up locally grown produce as well as homemade breads, pasta, honey, cheese, and more from over 100 vendors. You'll also find prepared foods you can purchase to make your life easier throughout the week. This market is held at Waterside, a popular lakeside dining and shopping destination. You'll often find food trucks as well as live music so you can make a day of the experience. Picnic tables are available under cover by the lake if you need to get out of the sun. Waterside also has plenty of public restrooms. Pick up that special gift from one of the local jewelry or fashion artisans and support locals. Friendly pets are always welcome. Arrive early for the free yoga class at 9 a.m. at Waterside Park. The market is open every Sunday from 10 a.m. to 2 p.m.

1561 Lakefront Dr., Lakewood Ranch
lakewoodranch.com/life-on-the-ranch/themarket

TIP

Bring a cooler with ice packs in case you decide to go to lunch after shopping.

MORE FARMERS MARKETS IN THE SARASOTA AREA

Most markets are only open one day per week and some take a break in the offseason, so be sure to check the website or give them a call before you head out.

Bradenton Market
400 Old Main St., Bradenton, 941-301-8445
realizebradenton.com/public-market

Fresh Harvest Farmers Market
19745 Wellen Pk. Blvd., Venice, 941-960-7805
wellenpark.com/events/fresh-harvest-farmers-market

Meadows Farmers Market
5041 Ringwood Meadow, Bldg. G-2, 941-315-7773
meadowsfarmersmarket.com

Phillippi Farmhouse Market
5500 S Tamiami Trl., 941-861-5000
farmhousemarket.org

Sarasota Farmers Market
N Lemon Ave., 941-225-9256
sarasotafarmersmarket.org

Siesta Key Farmers Market
5211 Ocean Blvd., Siesta Key
facebook.com/SiestaKeyFarmersMarket

Venice Farmers Market
401 W Venice Ave., Venice, 941-685-8196
thevenicefarmersmarket.org

FIND A GREAT READ
AT LOCAL BOOKSTORE1SARASOTA

Bookstores are not as popular as they once were, with online shopping being the preference of so many. Which is all the more reason for those of us who love printed works to support local booksellers. At Bookstore1Sarasota, located in the heart of the city since 2011, you can browse new books, hard-to-find books, used books, and even audiobooks. This independently owned bookstore offers a little bit of everything, from fiction and nonfiction to poetry, cookbooks, and local authors. Join a book club, visit for one of their live events, or listen to their book-lovers podcast. Don't know what you're looking for? Browse titles from the store's weekly Top 10 or annual Favorite Books of the Year lists. Looking for a gift? This shop has puzzles, greeting cards, and a handful of Florida-themed items. Bonus: they can all be gift wrapped at no cost with purchase.

And of course, you can always order online, but visiting in person is so much more fun!

117 S Pineapple Ave., 941-365-7900
sarasotabooks.com

TASTE YOUR WAY THROUGH TURKISH SWEETS AT EPHESUS MEDITERRANEAN DELIGHTS

With so many wonderful restaurants in St. Armands Circle, I'm sure many of them have amazing desserts. But this is my favorite dessert spot when I have dinner on St. Armands Circle. Stop in for a strong Turkish coffee and sip while you're browsing the incredible display of Turkish sweets. We're partial to the rose and pistachio, but everything behind the counter is delicious. Try the baklava! You can also pick up herbal teas, boxed candies, and even gift boxes. They also serve herbal teas and brewed coffee, as well as lattes and cappuccinos. Take a look around and you'll also find jewelry and other gifts items. We used to just stop by and purchase our treats to take home, but now we always sit for a bit and enjoy the atmosphere and some of our delicious candies. The store is charming, and the staff is always so kind.

27 N Blvd. of the Presidents, 352-217-3195
facebook.com/ephesusmediterraneandelights

100

PICK UP NECESSITIES
AT MORTON'S GOURMET MARKET

If this self-proclaimed foodie was visiting the area, Morton's would be my first stop after the airport. Marable's Market was Sarasota's first full-service grocery store. In 1969, Ted Morton bought the market, after working for the store for 17 years. As they say, the rest is history. And though it did change hands at one point, the Morton family owns Morton's Gourmet Market today. The cheese section has so many varieties, it would make any cheesemonger proud. Morton's even has Comté cheese, which is hard to come by in Florida and probably most other states. Pick up your charcuterie items here as they have all kinds of jams and spreads. Fresh breads, pastries, and desserts are in the smaller room just to the left as you enter the store. The deli, which is the heart of the store, has a plethora of salads you can take home along with freshly sliced deli items for sandwiches on the beach.

1924 S Osprey Ave., 941-955-9856
mortonsmarket.com

ACTIVITIES BY SEASON

SPRING

SUMMER

FALL

WINTER

Holidays at UTC

SUGGESTED ITINERARIES

DATE NIGHT

FAMILY FUN

FOODIES

HISTORY BUFFS

SPORTS FANS

ADVENTURERS

BEACH LOVERS

MUSIC LOVERS

RAINY DAY ADVENTURES

Ginny & Jane E's

INDEX

FISHING TACKLE AND HUNTING OUTFITS

Owens Fish Camp
Lakewood Ranch

Owen's Fish Camp